TABLE OF CONTENTS

D0123642

THE BEET GENERATION

Down-to-earth cooking varies from guru to gourmet. While basically vegetarian, it's a hang loose, flexible diet that adapts to many tastes. Even carnivorous parents like it.

You don't have to be young, long-haired, sandal-footed, or healthy, to dig the fresh flavor of down-to-earth, organic foods where grains are whole, fruit is for real, and vegetables are good enough to live on.

The vegetarian kitchen embraces several esoteric diets such as macrobiotic which is based on the yin and yang balance of cereals, selected vegetables, and other foods. There is also the vegetarian purist diet which excludes any animal by-products such as milk, egg, and cheese; and, the Tarzan-and-Jane raw fruits and vegetables diet for those who like their vitamins wild. However, down-to-earth cooking is principally designed for the garden variety vegetarian as well as the semi-vegan who goes along with a little organic chicken, fish, or shellfish occasionally.

Whatever food trip you're on, you'll find recipes in all chapters for every taste and conscience. We've gotten it all together—the yin and the yang, the raw and the cooked, the bland and the spicy, the vegetable and the semi-vegetable. (Many vegetable dishes have optional choices for chicken or seafood that can be added.)

We also include party food for friendly gatherings or hungry sensitivity groups; homemade breads and cakes that give you flour power; and far out picnics for rock festivals and other happenings. In addition, there is a chapter on the Down Home Kitchen with a shelf full of foods you can make yourself—from peanut butter to tortillas.

All ingredients in this book are organic and keyed to good nutrition: vegetable salt, or sea salt, is recommended over regular salt; raw sugar replaces refined white sugar, vegetable margarine is used in place of butter; flours are unbleached, and cereals are whole grain. In a kitchen where fresh is beautiful, canned or frozen foods are avoided whenever possible.

There's nothing new about down-to-earth cooking. It's been around since man discovered the plow. What's new is the generation that rediscovered it.

All recipes in this book are for 4 to 6 people—depending on appetites.

EVERYTHING YOU'VE ALWAYS WANTED TO KNOW ABOUT VEGETABLES

It takes a green thumb to raise vegetables, but a loving hand to cook them. Vegetables are easy to goof up if you don't know how to prepare them. Here are a few down-to-earth facts.

First, remember that organic produce raised without sprays or insecticides doesn't look as "flawless" as the commercial produce which has been dyed, sprayed, and beautified. With organic fruits and vegetables you're buying flavor and nutrition—not a centerpiece for your dining room table. However, organic vegetables should look crisp and fresh with a good natural color. If you buy them at the peak of their seasons, they're not only more flavorful, but cost less bread. Choose untrimmed vegetables with tops, or outside leaves, that can flavor the soup pot or salad bowl.

The sooner you store your vegetables in plastic bags or containers in the fridge, the longer they'll last. Light, air, and loss of moisture destroys all those vitamin goodies as well as flavor. Dry root vegetables, however, such as potatoes and onions, can be stored in any dark, cool place where air circulates.

Resist the urge to wash or cut up vegetables before you store them; they fare better au natural—all but lettuce, which is o.k. to rinse. Remove tops to root vegetables as moisture is drawn from the root to the leaf after it's harvested. Another tip; if you want to revive a wilted veg, put it on a rack in a container with about 1/8 inch of water in the bottom, and stick it in the fridge. It works unless the greenery is really beat.

When preparing vegetables, don't be a compulsive parer, peeler or scraper. Stay thy knife. The skin contains half, or more, of the flavor and nutrition of the vegetable. Arm yourself with a sturdy little scrub brush and scour away the dirt; rinse your greenery well *several* times in cold, running water. No soaking, please. That's a no-no vitamin-wise.

Slicing vegetables is an esoteric art in oriental countries where they cut them diagonally (*nituke* style) in thin matchstick strips suitable for quick stir-fry cooking. However you slice your vegetables, do it the last minute before cooking so they won't warm to room temperature.

The single most important thing to learn about vegetables is how to cook them. If you boil 'em, all the vital food elements—as well as flavors—dissolve in the cooking water. One of the best methods of vegetable cookery is the stir-fry where vegetables are briefly sauteed in a little oil—as is done in oriental and macrobiotic cooking. The second method, which we prefer for most basic vegetable cookery, is quick steaming. Vegetables emerge from the pot with a crisp tender texture and all the vitamins they were born with.

If you don't have a regular steamer (which is a good investment) you can use any large pot with a tight-fitting lid. Use a colander small enough to fit into the pot, or two foil pie tins which have been punched with holes. Invert one pie tin on the bottom of the pot and place the other on top right side up. Pour a few tablespoons of vegetable stock or water in the bottom of the pot and tightly close the lid. When the pot is full of steam, put the vegetables in the colander or pie tin. Close the lid and steam for 5 to 8 minutes if vegetables are cut, or 10 to 15 minutes if left whole. They should be tender but still a little crunchy. Better underdone than overdone, Confucius say.

Season your vegetables with margarine and salt, AFTER they're cooked, not before. Salt draws out moisture and natural juices—unless vegetables are cooked in a sauce.

Any left-overs should be quickly chilled. If you reheat cooked vegetables in a small amount of liquid, under a low temperature with all light excluded, you'll hang on to those vitamins—which is what it's all about.

This may be more than you ever wanted to know about vegetables—but it'll put you ahead of the jolly green giant!

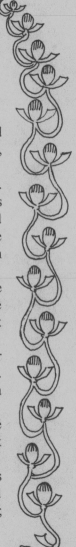

CHAPTER 1

KARMA KITCHEN

Karma is the moral consequence of one's deeds. In Buddhism and Hinduism, food is an important part of your karma. If you eat unwisely, you lose your wisdom as well as your waistline.

One of the most popular of the esoteric diets is the Zen macrobiotic. This diet is based on Japanese Zen cookery as practiced for centuries by Buddhist monks. In the macrobiotic regimen, foods are selected and prepared for spiritual as well as physical rejuvenation. Foods with more yin, or potassium, are eaten in proper balance, or ratio, to foods with more yang, or sodium.

While this diet emphasizes the wholesome properties of all whole grains—as well as selected fresh vegetables and fish—the principal staple is brown rice which has the ideal ratio of yin and yang, or perfect nourishment.

Macrobiotics aside, if you didn't know this diet was so good for your karma, you'd think it was unusually tasty food—so go ahead and try it. What's more, it's non-fattening. What other diet takes care of your karma as well as your calories?

This chapter is only a sampling of the Macrobiotic kitchen. If you're interested in pursuing this philosophy, there are several good paperback books on the subject.

The Tarmari soy sauce, soba noodles, and Japanese umeboshi plums listed in this chapter may be purchased at oriental markets, health food stores, and some supermarkets. The gomasio sesame salt is easy to make; the recipe is on page 88 .

Brown rice comes closest to the perfect ratio of five parts yin, or potassium, to 1 part yang, or sodium. With a beautiful ratio like this, it deserves proper cooking.

Rice should be cooked in a heavy pot with a tight-fitting lid. Wash the rice several times in cold water. Heat 2 Tbsp of corn oil in pot, and saute 1 cup of rice until grains are coated with oil. Pour in 2 1/2 cups water and season with 1/2 tsp sea salt. When water boils, cover and simmer rice for 45 minutes to an hour.

Rice is ready to serve when grains at the bottom of the pot are slightly scorched. The scorched part is very nutritious and very yang. This is the only kitchen in the world where you are rewarded for scorching the pot! But don't over-do it.

Let rice sit for 10 minutes before serving. This amount of rice will serve 2 people, more or less. Figure 2 cups for 4 people.

Buddha Bowl

Contemplate this beautiful blending of vegetables and rice.

8 broccoli flowerets
4 carrots, cut in quarters
8 summer squash, halved
4 zucchini, halved
1 tsp gomasio sesame salt
4 cups cooked brown rice
Cheddar cheese (optional)
Tarmari soy sauce

Steam broccoli, carrots, summer squash, and zucchini until crisp-tender, and season with gomasio salt.

Spoon 1 cup of hot brown rice into each of 4 small, oven-proof bowls. Top each bowl of rice with 2 broccoli flowerets, 4 quarters of carrot, 4 halves of summer squash, 2 halves of zucchini.

Since cheese is allowed occasionally in the macrobiotic diet, try a sprinkling of Cheddar cheese over the top of the rice. Put bowls under the broiler for a minute or two until cheese melts.

Tarmari soy sauce may be substituted for the cheese topping.

Baked Barley

Here's proof you can eat for pleasure as well as for principle.

4 Tbsp corn oil
2 cups green onions, chopped
1/2 cup green onion tops, chopped
1/4 cup green pepper, chopped
1/2 cup celery chopped
1 cup pearl barley
1/2 cup cooked, diced carrots

1/2 cup shelled pine nuts
5 cups vegetable stock
1 tsp gomasio sesame salt
1/2 clove garlic, minced
1/2 tsp marjoram
1/2 tsp basil
1 Tbsp parsley, chopped

Heat corn oil and saute green onions, onion tops, green pepper, and celery until vegetables are lightly cooked. Remove from skillet and saute barley until it turns golden brown in about 5 minutes.

Combine vegetables and barley with carrots and pine nuts in a casserole. Pour in 2 cups vegetable stock and season with gomasio salt, garlic, marjoram, basil, and parsley. Cover and bake 30 minutes at 350 degrees.

Carefully stir in 2 more cups of stock; cover and bake another 30 minutes. Add a 5th cup of stock, mixing well; and bake casserole uncovered for 15 minutes more.

After a hard day of meditation, reward yourself with this heavenly dish.

2 cups cooked, cold brown rice
1/2 lb sliced mushrooms, lightly sauteed
1/2 cup diced green pepper, lightly sauteed
1 cup water chestnuts, sliced
3 pimientos, sliced
1/4 cup parsley, chopped
1/4 cup green onions chopped
1/2 cup vegetable oil
1/2 tsp sea salt
1 Tbsp Tarmari soy sauce
3 Tbsp wine vinegar
2 tsp brown mustard

Combine cooked brown rice, mushrooms, green pepper, water chestnuts, pimientos, parsley, and green onions in a salad bowl.

Stir together vegetable oil, sea salt, soy sauce, wine vinegar, and
mustard. Pour dressing over rice and toss well.

This Umeboshi Plum Sauce has a delicate, slightly salty flavor which enhances fish as well as sauteed vegetables. Umeboshi salted plums turn up in a number of Japanese, or macrobiotic, dishes.

1 1/2 lbs fish fillets (perch, snapper,
   sole)
1/3 cup Umeboshi Plum Sauce
1 tsp Tarmari soy sauce
2 Tbsp toasted sesame seeds
1 Tbsp chopped parsley

Place fish fillets in greased pan.

Mix plum sauce with soy sauce and brush over fish.

Broil fish on both sides until it easily flakes with a fork, but do not overcook. Baste fish frequently with plum sauce mixture.

Sprinkle toasted sesame seeds and chopped parsley over fish before serving. Serve with brown rice.

UMEBOSHI PLUM SAUCE

3 umeboshi plums
1 cup water
1 Tbsp vegetable oil
1 Tbsp parsley, chopped
1 Tbsp leek, finely chopped
1/4 tsp sea salt

Boil plums in water for 10 minutes in a covered saucepan. Remove plums and reserve liquid. Pit plums and put into a blender with liquid. Blend until plums are pureed. Combine plum mixture with oil, parsley, leek, and sea salt. Briefly simmer sauce for 2 minutes.

The vibes and flavor are Indian.

1/2 cup corn oil
1 cup celery, diced
1 cup green pepper, diced
1/2 cup onion, grated
1 large green apple, grated
2 cups brown rice
5 cups vegetable stock
2 tsp sea salt
1/2 cup currants or raisins
2 tsp curry powder

Heat oil in saucepan and lightly saute celery, green pepper, onion, and apple. Remove vegetables and reserve. Add rice and lightly brown. Drain oil from pan and add vegetable stock and sea salt. Cover pan and cook rice for 45 minutes.

Stir in vegetables, currants, and curry powder.

Cover and cook an additional 15 to 20 minutes until rice is tender.

This is a variation of a dish called "Food for the Saints" since it is eaten by the Arhats, or Buddhist Saints. While it is Chinese, the principle is Macrobiotic.

1/4 cup green onions,	1/2 cup Chinese peas, whole
1/4 cup mushrooms	1 cup bean sprouts
1/4 cup celery	1/4 cup water
1/2 cup broccoli	1 Tbsp arrowroot
1/2 cup water chestnuts	2 Tbsp Tarmari soy sauce
1/2 cup carrots	1/2 tsp sugar
1/2 cup zucchini	Gomasio salt to taste
4 Tbsp vegetable oil	1 cup bean curd, cut in small pieces

1 cup Chinese or American cabbage, shredded

Cut the following vegetables nituke, or oriental style, in thin diagonal strips: green onions, mushrooms, celery, broccoli, water chestnuts, carrots, and zucchini.

Heat oil in a Chinese Wok, or large skillet, and add all vegetables including cabbage, peas, and bean sprouts. Stir fry vegetables for 2 or 3 minutes. Add water, arrowroot, soy sauce, sugar, and gomasio salt to taste, and stir. Add bean curd which has been briefly browned on both sides.

Cover Wok, or skillet, and simmer 5 minutes. Take off lid and stir fry for another minute or two. Serve over hot brown rice.

For gourmet gurus: an inspired vegetable curry. One of the secrets of this curry is a touch of guava jelly. The vegetables are equally good over brown rice, as well as kasha.

1/2 cup fresh shelled peas
1 cup carrots, diced
2 cups summer squash, diced
1/2 cup celery, diced
1 cup broccoli, broken into
   flowerets and sliced
4 Tbsp corn oil
1/2 cup onion, finely chopped
2 tsp curry powder

2 Tbsp wholewheat pastry flour
1 Tbsp guava jelly
1 tsp lime juice
1 1/2 cups vegetable stock
2 Tbsp corn oil
1/2 cup kasha (buckwheat groats)
2 cups water
1/2 tsp sea salt

Steam peas, carrots, summer squash, celery, and broccoli until crisp-tender.

Heat corn oil and saute onion until tender. Add curry powder and flour and mix well. Stir in guava jelly and lime juice; and simmer for a moment. Gradually add vegetable stock and simmer until sauce thickens before adding steamed vegetables. Simmer vegetables until hot.

Saute kasha in corn oil for a few minutes. Add water and salt; when water boils, lower flame, cover pot, and simmer kasha for 15 to 20 minutes.

Spoon the vegetable curry over the kasha before serving.

Zen Noodles with Sauteed Vegetables 18

Japanese soba noodles are the healthiest noodles in the world. These are made of buckwheat and are very nourishing. The accent of plum sauce is most savory.

3 Tbsp corn oil
2 large onions, thinly sliced
4 green onions, thinly sliced
4 carrots, thinly sliced
1 cup cauliflower, broken into
   flowerets and sliced

1/2 head cabbage, shredded
1 tsp gomasio sesame salt
*5 Tbsp Umeboshi Plum Sauce
1 package buckwheat soba noodles
1 tsp sea salt
3 qts boiling water

Heat oil in a skillet and saute onions, green onions, carrots, and cauliflower for a few minutes. Add cabbage and saute until vegetables are lightly cooked. Season with gomasio salt, add Umeboshi Plum Sauce, cover skillet, and simmer vegetables another 10 minutes. Keep warm.

Add soba noodles to boiling, salted water. When water returns to a boil, add a little cold water to stop the boiling. When it comes to a boil again, test noodles to see if they are soft. If not, add a little more cold water and let noodles remain in hot water—without boiling—until they are cooked. Remove from stove, drain, and quickly rinse noodles under cold water.

Combine noodles, vegetables, and vegetable liquid in a pot; and briefly re-heat. We like to stir in 2 or 3 Tbsp of margarine just before serving. It isn't Zen, but it's tasty.

*See recipe for Umeboshi Plum Sauce on page 14.

The following four recipes are dedicated to those on a raw food diet. While this diet has nothing to do with macrobiotic, we decided to include these recipes in Karma Kitchen since the raw food regimen is also esoteric and purifying. Most of these foods can be enjoyed on a macrobiotic diet—with a few substitutions here and there.

Avocado and Bean Sprouts

2 large avocados
Lemon or lime juice
1/4 cup honey
1/4 cup sour cream
3 Tbsp salad dressing
1/4 cup green onions, thinly sliced
1 Tbsp parsley, chopped

1/2 tsp garlic salt
1/8 tsp ground ginger
1/4 lb fresh bean sprouts
1/4 cup celery, thinly sliced
1/4 cup water chestnuts, sliced
Salad greens

Peel and halve avocados and remove pits. Drizzle lemon or lime juice over avocados.

Combine honey with sour cream, salad dressing, green onions, parsley, garlic salt, and ginger; stir until well blended.

Rinse bean sprouts and pat dry with paper towels. Chop sprouts slightly and put into a bowl. Add celery and water chestnuts. Toss well with honey-sour cream dressing.

Put avocado halves on a bed of salad greens, and spoon bean sprouts over avocados.

Raw Vegetables and Fruit Salad 20

A salad that gets it all together: vitamins, vegetables, fruit, and flavor.

1 cup fresh spinach, finely chopped
1 cup cabbage, finely chopped
1 cup celery, finely chopped
3 green onions, finely chopped
2 fresh peaches, pared and sliced
2 fresh pears, pared and sliced
2 apples, pared, cored, and chopped
1/2 cup walnuts, chopped

Mix vegetables, fruits, and walnuts together. Toss well with a French dressing, or any of your favorite salad dressings.

For variation, try these other salad combinations:

Sprouted wheat, chopped green onions, chopped celery, and parsley.

Carrots, celery root, and watercress.

Celery, apples, dates, figs, and nuts.

Grated endive, raw peeled beets, cashew nuts, bean sprouts, and parsley.

Shredded Swiss chard, grated carrots, and chopped green onions.

Sages say that foods with an ancient origin widen one's scope of thinking. There's no food older or wiser than the apple!

1 large red onion, thinly sliced
3 large, tart apples, cored, pared, and thinly sliced
2 cucumbers, peeled, and thinly sliced
3 or 4 slices pimiento
1/2 cup vegetable oil
1/4 cup lime or lemon juice
1 tsp sea salt
1/2 clove garlic, crushed
1 cup cooked coarsely grated chestnuts

Combine onion, apples, cucumbers, and pimiento in a salad bowl. Mix together vegetable oil, lime or lemon juice, sea salt, and garlic. Pour over salad and marinate 1 hour.

Sprinkle hot grated chestnuts over salad before serving.

Everything here is raw but the peanuts—which are much tastier if lightly roasted. However, if you're a purist, go ahead and use them raw.

2 cups celery, chopped
1/2 cup carrots, chopped
1 cup ground peanuts
1/2 cup cabbage, finely shredded
2 very ripe avocados, peeled and mashed
3 Tbsp onion, grated
2 Tbsp parsley, minced
1 tsp thyme
1/2 tsp rubbed sage
1/2 tsp pepper
2 tsp salt
Juice of 1 lemon

Remove strings from celery and combine with carrots. Put vegetables into blender—a little at a time.

Lightly roast peanuts, following recipe on page 103 or leave them raw.

Grind nuts, and combine in a bowl with carrots, celery, cabbage, avocados, onion, parsley, thyme, sage, pepper, salt, and lemon juice. Mix well and shape into a loaf.

Serve on salad greens.

GETTING IT ALL TOGETHER

There are more varieties of vegetarians than you can shake a carrot at. Some are purists who take their vegetables straight; others are gourmets who embellish their greenery with sauces and herbs. There are also the quasi-vegetarians who occasionally sneak a little chicken or seafood into their diet.

However varied, vegetarians share a friendly way of eating—and living. While we can't proclaim that vegans are more cosmic than carnivores, maybe a herbivorous diet takes a little of the growl out of life.

This chapter brings together vegetarian dishes to delight all tastes. There are vegetable specialties and savory casseroles to stimulate the imagination and cool the economy. And for the semi-vegan, optional choices are indicated in recipes where chicken or shellfish may be added.

Super Beans

When green beans get together with water chestnuts, mushrooms, and sour cream, they're really super.

1 1/2 lb green beans
2 tsp vegetable salt
1 1/2 cups sour cream
1 Tbsp wholewheat pastry flour
3/4 cup cooked, small white onions
1/2 cup water chestnuts, sliced
1/2 cup cooked mushrooms, sliced
3 Tbsp pimientos, chopped
3/4 cup Cheddar cheese, grated

Wash beans and cut off tips; break beans into 2-inch lengths. Steam beans until they are crisp tender. Drain and season with vegetable salt. Mix beans with sour cream, flour, white onions, water chestnuts, mushrooms, and pimientos.

Spoon vegetables into a casserole and sprinkle with Cheddar cheese. Cover and bake in a 350 degree oven for 20 minutes.

Avocado makes a dip, salad, butter, soup, ice cream, drink, and sandwich—as well as a fabulous dinner-on-the-half-shell.

1/4 cup margarine
1 apple, pared, cored, and chopped
1 small onion, chopped
1 clove garlic, crushed
1 Tbsp (or more) curry
1/4 cup wholewheat pastry flour
1 cup light cream

1 cup chicken stock or milk
1 tsp salt
1/8 tsp white pepper
2 cups cooked mixed vegetables, cut in small chunks
4 avocados, halved and peeled
3 cups cooked brown rice

Melt margarine in a saucepan, and saute apple, onion, and garlic for 10 minutes until onion and apple are soft and tender. Stir in curry powder and flour, and simmer 1 minute. Gradually add cream and chicken stock, or milk. (Chicken stock is preferable in a curry sauce if you're not a strict vegetarian.) Stir sauce until it thickens and add salt, pepper, and vegetables. Increase curry according to taste. Simmer sauce for 10 minutes.

Spoon cooked brown rice in a casserole and place avocado halves on top of rice. Heat casserole in oven for 5 minutes—or just long enough to warm avocados; do not overcook. Spoon curried vegetables into avocado halves and serve with condiments of chopped eggs, coconut, raisins, peach chutney and chopped peanuts.

Optional: Cooked, boned & skinned chicken, or cooked shrimp, may be used in place of vegetables.

Country soup is folk art. This one has the lively seasonings of Italy.

1 cup navy beans or kidney beans
6 cups vegetable stock
1/2 tsp salt
1 clove garlic, minced
1 onion, chopped
2 Tbsp parsley, chopped
1/2 cup celery, chopped

1 cup tomatoes, diced
1 cup cabbage, coarsely chopped
*1 cup cooked Vegeroni
1/2 tsp paprika
salt to taste
Parmesan cheese, grated

Wash beans and put in a large saucepan with water to cover. Bring water to a boil and simmer beans for 2 minutes. Remove from stove and let beans soak for 1 hour.

Drain beans and add vegetable stock; simmer for 1 hour. Add salt, garlic, onion, parsley, celery and tomatoes. Simmer another 1/2 hour and add cabbage, Vegeroni, paprika, and additional salt if needed. Simmer 1/2 hour.

Ladle soup into soup bowls and top with a generous sprinkling of Parmesan cheese before serving.

*This vegetable-flavored macaroni may be purchased at health food stores and some markets. Regular macaroni may be substituted if you like.

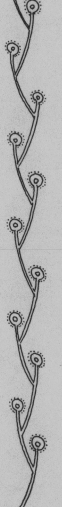

For broccoli buffs who are looking for new ways to cook their favorite greenery.

1 1/2 lb broccoli	1/4 tsp white pepper
1/4 cup margarine	2 Tbsp dry sherry
5 Tbsp wholewheat pastry flour	1 tsp lemon juice
1 cup milk	1 tsp fine herbs
1 cup cream	1/4 tsp paprika
1 cup Gruyere or Cheddar cheese, grated	1/4 cup Parmesan cheese, grated
	1/4 cup wholewheat bread crumbs
1 tsp salt	1/4 cup chopped pistachio nuts

Steam broccoli until tender. Break into flowerets.

Melt margarine in a skillet and stir in flour. Gradually add hot milk and cream, and stir until sauce thickens. Add cheese and stir until cheese melts. Season sauce with salt, pepper, sherry, lemon juice, herbs, and paprika.

Spoon drained broccoli into a baking dish and pour over sauce. Sprinkle with Parmesan cheese and bread crumbs, and top with pistachio nuts. Bake in a 350 degree oven for 10 to 15 minutes.

Optional: Add 1 cup of cooked shellfish to mornay sauce; or, layer 4 lightly sauteed fish fillets on top of broccoli before spooning over sauce.

Starving Artists' Macaroni

You don't have to be an artist to enjoy this macaroni pie—but it helps if you're starving. It's a nourishing dish.

1/4 cup margarine
1 1/2 cups light cream, scalded
1 cup soft wholewheat bread crumbs
2 Tbsp chopped green pepper
1 Tbsp onion, grated
1/2 tsp dry mustard
1 cup Cheddar cheese, grated
1 tsp salt
1/2 tsp pepper
1 Tbsp parsley, minced
1 Tbsp pimiento, minced
1 cup cooked macaroni
3 large eggs, beaten

Melt margarine in a skillet and stir in scalded cream, bread crumbs, green pepper, and grated onion. Dissolve mustard in 1 Tbsp water and add to skillet. Stir in Cheddar cheese, salt, pepper, parsley, pimiento, and macaroni. Cook until lukewarm. Add beaten eggs and blend well.

Pour mixture into a greased casserole. Place casserole in a pan of hot water and bake in a 375 degree oven for 45 minutes or until done.

Serve with Fresh Mushroom Sauce (page 93).

Have you ever had your favorite thistle with cream cheese sauce?

4 large artichokes
4 Tbsp wine vinegar
3 Tbsp olive oil
2 bay leaves
2 tsp vegetable salt
2 Tbsp tarragon vinegar
2 Tbsp green onions, minced

1/2 tsp tarragon
6 oz cream cheese
1 Tbsp chives, chopped
3 Tbsp lime juice
1/2 cup Parmesan cheese, grated
light cream

Slice 1/2 inch off top of artichokes. Cut off stems, and pull off small leaves at the base of the artichokes. Place vegetables in large pot of boiling water sufficient to cover artichokes, and add vinegar, olive oil, bay leaves, and salt. Cover and simmer for 45 minutes or until artichokes are tender. Drain. Gently push aside center leaves and remove feathery choke with a spoon.

In a saucepan combine tarragon vinegar, green onions, and tarragon; simmer until vinegar evaporates. Add cream cheese, chives, lime juice, and Parmesan cheese; and mash ingredients together with a fork. Stir until cheese melts and sauce is smooth and hot. Thin sauce with a little cream until it is the right consistency to be used as a dip. Pour sauce into the hollowed-out section of artichokes before serving.

Optional: As an alternate filling, try this brown rice stuffing. Combine 1 cup cooked brown rice with 1 cup cooked chopped chicken (or 1 cup cooked shellfish), and 1/4 cup sauteed green onions, 1/4 cup sauteed green pepper, and 1 1/2 cups grated Cheddar cheese.

Lemon Carrots and Apples

Even carrot-haters like this. The apples and touch-of-lemon add a yummy flavor.

6 carrots, thinly sliced
2 green apples, cored and thinly sliced
2 tsp grated lemon peel
3 Tbsp margarine, melted
1 tsp vegetable salt
1/2 cup Cheddar cheese, grated

Arrange carrots and apples in alternate layers in a steamer. Sprinkle with lemon peel. Steam until crisp-tender. Transfer to a serving dish. Pour margarine over carrots and apples, and season with vegetable salt. Stir in Cheddar cheese before serving.

Try this with cooked brown rice or millet.

An easy going dish that expands into a dinner with the addition of chicken; or serves as a zesty side dish with vegetables. Increase or decrease the amount of chilies according to taste.

1 1/2 cups sour cream
2 Tbsp green chili peppers, seeded and diced
3 cups cooked brown rice
1/2 lb Jack cheese, cut in strips
1/2 cup Cheddar cheese, grated

Mix sour cream with green chilies.

Put a layer of brown rice in the bottom of a small greased casserole. Spoon 3/4 of a cup of sour cream mixture over rice. Lay 1/2 of the Jack cheese strips over the top. Make another layer of rice, sour cream, and cheese strips, ending with a final layer of rice on top. Sprinkle top with Cheddar cheese. Cover and bake for 20 minutes until cheese melts.

Optional: Layer small pieces of cooked, boneless chicken between the sour cream mixture and Jack cheese.

This tastes more like pasta more than potatoes. Don't count the calories —relax and enjoy.

3 large potatoes, peeled and
   quartered
1 cup wholewheat pastry flour
1 tsp salt
1/2 tsp pepper
1/4 cup olive oil
3 Tbsp margarine
3 Tbsp wholewheat pastry flour
3 large, ripe tomatoes, chopped
1/2 green pepper, chopped

1 small onion, finely chopped
1 Tbsp raw sugar
1 tsp vegetable salt
1/2 bay leaf
2 cloves
1/2 lb Mozzarella cheese, diced
1/4 cup Parmesan cheese, grated
1 Tbsp fresh oregano or 1 tsp
   dried oregano

Boil potatoes and mash until smooth. Mix in flour and blend well; season with salt & pepper.

Press potato mixture in a 1/2 inch thick layer in the bottom of a greased shallow baking dish. Spoon olive oil over top.

Melt margarine in a skillet and stir in flour. Add tomatoes, green pepper, onions, sugar, salt, bay leaf, and cloves. Simmer for 15 to 20 minutes. Remove bay leaf and cloves. Spoon tomato sauce over potato mixture.

Top pie with Mozzarella cheese and Parmesan cheese. Sprinkle with oregano. Bake in a 350 degree oven for 15 minutes or until top is lightly browned and bubbling.

We give you a nut loaf that doesn't taste like mock roast beef, substitute hamburger, or imitation meat loaf. It tastes like nut loaf—great!

1 1/2 cups ground nuts (pecans, almonds, walnuts, pine nuts, peanuts)
1 1/2 cups celery, ground
1/2 onion, ground
1 3/4 cups wholewheat bread crumbs
2 tsp salt
2 tsp curry powder
1/2 tsp onion salt
3 eggs, beaten
3 Tbsp margarine, melted
2 1/4 cups milk

Combine ground nuts with celery and onion. Add bread crumbs, salt, curry, onion salt, eggs, margarine, and milk. Mix well and let stand 20 minutes.

Pour mixture into a casserole, cover with foil and bake for 25 minutes at 375 degrees.

Uncover, and bake 25 minutes more at 400 degrees. Serve with Mushroom Sauce on page 93.

A popular dish with artists, surfers, street people, coupon clippers—and everybody else in Laguna Beach, California

1 cup green onions, chopped
1/2 cup celery, sliced
1/2 cup green pepper strips
2 Tbsp margarine or soy butter
2 cups cooked brown rice
2 tomatoes, quartered
1 cup Cheddar cheese, grated
1 small bunch parsley, finely chopped
1/4 clove garlic, finely chopped
2 tsp salt
1/2 tsp ground black pepper

Saute green onions, celery and green pepper in margarine (or soy butter) for 3 minutes—or until vegetables are barely tender.

Combine vegetables in a bowl with the hot brown rice, tomatoes, Cheddar cheese, parsley, garlic, salt and pepper. Mix well, allowing time for cheese to melt a little before serving.

Asparagus Letters

Try this novel way of steaming asparagus in foil envelopes—you'll get the message.

1 1/4 lb asparagus
1 lb fresh peas, shelled
1 cup lettuce, shredded
1 green onion, thinly sliced
6 Tbsp margarine
2 tsp vegetable salt
1/2 tsp ground black pepper

Cut off tough ends of asparagus. Wash tips well and thinly slice stalks diagonally.

In a bowl combine peas, lettuce, and green onion with asparagus. Mix well. Place 2/3 cup of mixed vegetables in the center of a 7 inch square of foil paper. Bring up sides of foil paper and fold over top securely making a tight packet. Wrap remaining vegetables the same way; each packet serves 1 person.

Arrange packets in a steamer with 1 inch of boiling water on bottom of steamer. Cover and steam for 30 minutes. Open packets and put 1 Tbsp of margarine in each packet of vegetables; and season with salt & pepper before serving.

Stuffed Cabbage with Soybeans

1 cup dry soybeans
1 tsp salt
3 tsp vegetable oil
1 Tbsp onion, minced
3/4 cup tomato puree
2 vegetable bouillon cubes
1 tsp soy sauce
1/2 cup celery, finely chopped
1/2 cup onion, finely chopped
2 Tbsp vegetable oil

1 Tbsp fine herbs
1 tsp salt
1/2 tsp pepper
1 tsp soy sauce
1 Tbsp Worcestershire Sauce
2 eggs, beaten
1 cup wheat germ
8 large cabbage leaves
*Vine Ripe Tomato Sauce

Soak soybeans overnight in enough salted water to cover. Drain and grind them in a food chopper. Transfer beans to a saucepan, add 2 cups water and simmer for 30 minutes or until they lose their raw taste.

Heat oil in a skillet and lightly brown onion. Add tomato puree, vegetable bouillon cubes, soy sauce, and cooked ground soybeans. Simmer beans until liquid almost evaporates.

Saute celery and onion in oil and add herbs, salt, pepper, soy sauce, and Worcestershire Sauce. Combine with beans. Stir in eggs and wheat germ and mix well.

Steam cabbage leaves for 3 or 5 minutes until tender. Drain. Spoon about 1/2 cup of bean mixture in the center of each cabbage leaf and fold over the leaf into a compact packet.

Place stuffed cabbage in a pan and spoon over a little Vine Ripe Tomato Sauce. Bake, uncovered, for 1 hour in a 350 degree oven. Baste frequently with the sauce.

*For recipe, see page 96.

Noodles with broccoli? Yes, and it's nifty.

8 oz cooked noodles
1/2 lb Swiss cheese, grated
2 cups fresh cooked broccoli, chopped
1/4 cup green onions, chopped
3 Tbsp butter
3 Tbsp wholewheat pastry flour
1 1/2 cups milk
1 tsp salt
1/2 tsp paprika
1/8 tsp white pepper
3 Tbsp margarine
1 Tbsp poppy seeds

Place 1/2 of the cooked noodles in the bottom of a greased casserole. Sprinkle with 1/2 of the Swiss cheese. Spoon over all of the broccoli and green onions.

Melt butter in a skillet and stir in flour. Gradually add milk and season with salt, paprika, and white pepper. Simmer and stir until sauce thickens. Pour 1/2 of the sauce over broccoli and onions. Spoon remaining noodles over top and cover with remaining sauce. Sprinkle with remaining cheese. Dot top with margarine and sprinkle with poppy seeds.

Bake for 20 minutes in a 350 degree oven.

Optional: A layer of cooked, boned chicken enriches this dish.

Cracked Wheat with Sour Cream

This dish takes on any cooked vegetables you want to add. Serve it hot or cold.

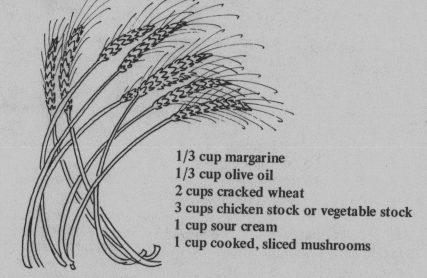

1/3 cup margarine
1/3 cup olive oil
2 cups cracked wheat
3 cups chicken stock or vegetable stock
1 cup sour cream
1 cup cooked, sliced mushrooms

Heat margarine and olive oil in a saucepan. Saute cracked wheat until golden brown, stirring constantly. Add chicken or vegetable stock, cover saucepan and simmer for 30 minutes stirring occasionally.

When wheat is cooked, remove pan from stove, and stir in sour cream and mushrooms.

Mixed Summer Squash

A potpourri of squashes in a tasty sour cream sauce.

1 1/2 lb mixed squash (summer squash, crookneck, and zucchini)
1/3 cup onions, finely chopped
3 Tbsp water
3 Tbsp margarine, melted
1 tsp vegetable salt
1/2 tsp black pepper
1 cup sour cream
1 tsp dill weed
2 Tbsp wholewheat pastry flour

Wash squash, and trim off ends. Cut into 1/2 inch slices.

Spoon squash and onions in the bottom of a greased casserole. Add water and tightly cover. Bake for 20 to 30 minutes until vegetables are crisp tender. Drain well. Pour over margarine and season with vegetable salt & black pepper.

In a bowl combine sour cream, dill weed, and flour. Stir sour cream mixture into squash. Bake, uncovered, for 15 minutes at 350 degrees.

Hobbit Mushroom Pudding

Only the hobbits could have invented this unbelievably good pudding.

3 Tbsp margarine
1/2 cup green onions, finely
   chopped
1/2 cup celery, finely chopped
5 cups mushrooms, coarsely
   chopped
2 Tbsp lemon juice
1 cup toasted wholewheat bread cubes

1/2 cup cooked brown rice
1/4 cup freshly grated Parmesan
   cheese
2 cups milk
4 eggs, beaten
1 tsp salt
1/4 tsp thyme

Melt margarine in a skillet and saute onions, celery, and mushrooms for 5 minutes. Stir in lemon juice and mix well. Cool.

Combine bread cubes, rice, and Parmesan cheese; and stir into vegetable mixture. Spoon into a greased baking dish.

Beat together milk, eggs, salt, and thyme; and pour over vegetable mixture. Place baking dish in a pan of hot water in a 325 degree oven and bake pudding, uncovered, for 45 minutes.

Optional: This pudding is also delicious with the addition of 1/2 cup of cooked chicken or shellfish.

If "cauliflower is nothing but cabbage with a college education," this cauliflower has a Ph.D.

1 large head cauliflower, broken into flowerets
4 large, ripe tomatoes, chopped
1 tsp basil
1 tsp oregano
2 tsp vegetable salt
2 Tbsp olive oil
1/2 cup green onions, thinly sliced
1/2 cup celery, thinly sliced
1/2 tsp celery salt
1/2 tsp black pepper
3 Tbsp parsley chopped
3/4 cup Parmesan cheese, finely grated

Steam cauliflower until barely tender, about 8 minutes. Drain and place in casserole.

Simmer tomatoes for 15 minutes in a saucepan with basil, oregano, vegetable salt, olive oil, green onions, celery, celery salt, and black pepper. Pour over cauliflower and sprinkle with parsley.

Cover casserole and bake in a 350 degree oven for 15 minutes. Sprinkle with Parmesan cheese and bake, uncovered, for 5 minutes more. Serve with, or over, homemade noodles.

Sauteed Bean Sprouts

Have you tried bean sprouts with an accent of sweet gherkins? Don't panic, it's great! Make sure, however, you use the very small, hors d'oeuvre size gherkins. No kosher pickles, please!

1 1/2 lb fresh bean sprouts
1 garlic clove finely chopped
2 slices fresh ginger, grated, or 1/4 tsp ground ginger
1 Tbsp corn oil
2 green onions, including tops, sliced
3 tiny sweet gherkins, thinly sliced
1 tsp sugar
3 Tbsp soy sauce
1/2 cup vegetable or chicken stock
1/8 tsp salt
2 Tbsp dry sherry
Toasted sesame seeds

Rinse bean sprouts well and pick out any husks. Drain and dry.
Lightly brown garlic and ginger in corn oil; add green onions, gherkins, sugar, soy sauce, vegetable or chicken stock, and bean sprouts. Simmer 3 minutes. Add 1/8 tsp salt and 2 Tbsp sherry. Mix well and cook a minute longer. Top with toasted sesame seeds before serving.

Green Corn Tamale Casserole

In Mexico they grind the green or fresh corn in a stone metate the same way the Aztecs did. You can get the same results with a blender—so cheat a little!

> 12 ears fresh corn
> 2 tsp salt
> 3 Tbsp margarine, melted
> 1 to 1 1/2 cups cornmeal
> 1/2 lb sharp Cheddar cheese, sliced
> 3 green chilies, seeded, deveined and cut in strips

Shuck corn, reserving husks. Cut kernels from corn cobs. Grind kernels in a blender until pureed. Add salt and margarine. Pour pureed corn into a bowl, and add sufficient cornmeal to make a mixture that can be easily spread. Mixture should not be too dry or stiff.

Line the bottom and sides of a casserole with green corn husks, leaving tips of husks standing above the rim of casserole. Spoon a layer of corn mixture on the bottom, and top with slices of Cheddar cheese and strips of green chiles. (while we customarily don't recommend canned products, the canned variety are good.) Spoon another layer of corn mixture, cheese, and chiles into casserole and top with the cornmeal. Fold corn husks extending above rim of casserole over the top of the dish, and cover casserole with foil paper. Bake in a 350 degree oven for 1 hour.

This is a nifty dish to serve with tacos or any Mexican goodie. If you like a milder flavor, use less chilies.

HAVE A NICE EVENING

Coming together means sharing ideas, cool wine, and whatever is in the oven. Pot luck is part of the scene. The nicest evenings are jointly made—one friend brings the spaghetti sauce, the other the harmonica. It is a time for rapping and getting it all together.

While most gatherings are spontaneous, some are special gigs you plan. We have festive food for both—everything from Mexican and Italian feasts to one-burner dinners.

All these dishes spread a lot of happiness for little bread.

Middle Kingdom Vegetable Dish   45

A vegetable banquet that is out of this world.

1 cup carrots, thinly sliced
1 cup green beans, cut into 1/2
  lengths
1 cup potatoes, diced
1/2 cup celery, sliced
2 tomatoes, cut in quarters
1 crookneck squash, thinly sliced
1 zucchini, thinly sliced
1/2 onion, thinly sliced
1/2 head cauliflower, cut into
  flowerets

1/4 cup sweet red pepper, thinly
  sliced
1/2 cup fresh green peas
1 cup vegetable stock
1/3 cup olive oil
2 cloves garlic, chopped
1/2 bay leaf
1/2 tsp tarragon
2 tsp vegetable salt
1/2 cup Parmesan cheese grated
Sliced Jack cheese

Combine in a shallow baking dish the carrots, green beans, potatoes, celery, tomatoes, squash, zucchini, onion, cauliflower, red pepper, and green peas.

Heat vegetable stock and combine with olive oil, garlic, bay leaf, and tarragon. Pour over vegetables. Tightly cover baking dish with foil before putting on lid. This seals the pot and prevents evaporation of the stock.

Bake in a 350 degree oven for 45 minutes or until vegetables are tender but still crisp. During baking, gently stir vegetables a few times.

Before serving, season with vegetable salt. Sprinkle top with Parmesan cheese and cover with slices of Jack cheese. Place baking dish under broiler until cheese melts.

Jack Cheese Tacos

All tacos aren't made with hamburger. Here's one with cheese topped with a zesty tomato sauce and sour cream. Olé!

2 green chilies, seeded and chopped	1/4 tsp sugar
3 large ripe tomatoes, diced	2 Tbsp vegetable oil
1 small onion, chopped	1 cup vegetable oil
2 tsp vegetable salt	8 corn tortillas
1/2 tsp black pepper	1/2 lb Jack cheese
	Sour cream

Combine chilies, tomatoes, and onion in a blender. Blend for a few minutes until ingredients are pureed. Add salt, pepper, and sugar. Add oil, and simmer sauce in a saucepan for 10 minutes, stirring frequently.

Heat 1 cup oil in a small skillet. When oil is hot, put in a tortilla. As soon as it becomes limp, fold tortilla in half using tongs. Insert tongs between folds of tortilla for a few seconds keeping edges apart until it becomes crisp. Turn tortilla over and lightly cook on other side for 10 seconds or so. Drain tortillas on paper towels as they are cooked, and keep warm.

Place a thick strip of Jack cheese inside each tortilla and spoon a few tablespoons of tomato sauce over cheese. Top with a generous dab of sour cream.

Serve tacos with a platter of supplementary fillings such as shredded lettuce, avocado slices, sliced tomatoes, and Cheddar cheese strips.

Optional: Chicken is also a tasty addition to this taco. Use cooked breast of chicken which has been skinned, boned, and shredded.

We're putting in this recipe at the risk of being dropped by the counter-culture. This spinach is establishment—but it's fabulous.

1 1/2 lb fresh spinach, finely chopped
1 tsp vegetable salt
1/4 tsp pepper
1 egg yolk, beaten
1/4 cup heavy cream
2 cups bechamel sauce
1/2 cup grated Gruyere or Parmesan cheese
1 cup fresh mushrooms, sauteed
1/4 cup toasted almonds, sliced

Steam spinach a few minutes until tender. Press out excess water. Season with vegetable salt and pepper.

Blend egg yolk with cream and stir into 2 cups bechamel sauce. (See page 92.) Add cheese and stir until cheese melts; do not boil.

Put spinach in a baking dish and spoon over mushrooms. Pour sauce over top. Sprinkle with toasted almonds. Bake in a 350 degree oven for 10 minutes or until top is golden brown.

Optional: Layer 4 lightly broiled fillets of sole over spinach before covering with mushrooms and sauce. Bake 10 minutes.

Eggplant with Yogurt

Here's a nifty dish for student parties where the kitchen is a two-burner stove, or electric skillet, and the cooking is casual.

1 onion, finely chopped
2 Tbsp margarine
4 ripe tomatoes, diced
1 Tbsp sugar
1 tsp fresh ginger root, chopped,
  or 1/2 tsp ginger powder
1 1/2 tsp vegetable salt
1/4 tsp black pepper

1 large eggplant, cut in slices 3/4
  inch thick
1/2 cup vegetable oil
1 tsp vegetable salt
1/2 tsp pepper
1 cup yogurt or sour cream
2 Tbsp parsley, finely chopped

Saute onion in margarine until golden brown. Add tomatoes, and season with sugar, ginger, vegetable salt, and pepper. Simmer, uncovered, until sauce thickens in about 10 minutes.

Dip eggplant slices in oil, coating each side well. Arrange eggplant in a single layer in an electric skillet, or regular skillet, and simmer over a low heat for 30 minutes or until tender. Turn eggplant occasionally so it's nicely browned on both sides. Season with salt & pepper.

Place eggplant slices on a serving dish and spoon yogurt or sour cream over the top of each slice. Top with a few tablespoons of tomato sauce in the center of each slice, leaving a border of yogurt or sour cream. Garnish with parsley. Serve over, or with, brown rice.

Groovy Green Beans

A green bean supper for the blue jean generation.

1 lb green beans, cut in 2 inch lengths
1/4 cup margarine
1/4 cup onion, finely chopped
1/4 cup wholewheat pastry flour
2 cups milk
2 tsp salt
1/2 tsp black pepper
1/2 tsp thyme
1/2 tsp savory
1 Tbsp parsley, chopped
6 hard-cooked eggs, sliced
1/4 cup wholewheat bread crumbs
1/2 cup Swiss cheese, grated

Steam green beans until tender crisp. Drain.

Melt margarine in a skillet and saute onions until tender. Remove from heat and stir in flour. Return skillet to stove and gradually add milk, stirring until sauce thickens. Season with salt, pepper, thyme, savory, and parsley. Simmer 2 minutes.

Layer beans, egg slices, and sauce in a casserole. Combine bread crumbs with cheese, and sprinkle over top.

Bake for 20 minutes in a 350 degree oven.

Homemade lasagna is the secret here. Make the lasagna well in advance to give it time to dry out slightly before cooking.

1/4 cup olive oil	4 cups unbleached white flour
2 onions, finely chopped	1 tsp salt
2 cups tomato puree	3/4 cup spinach puree
2 tsp vegetable salt	2 eggs, beaten
1/2 tsp pepper	1/2 lb Mozzarella cheese, thinly
1 tsp oregano	sliced
1 tsp basil	1 cup freshly grated Parmesan cheese

Heat oil in skillet, and saute onions for 5 minutes. Add tomato puree, salt, pepper, oregano, and basil. Cover and simmer over low heat for 40 minutes. Add a little water if sauce becomes too thick.

Sift flour and salt together in a mixing bowl. Make a well in the center and pour in spinach puree and eggs. Mix well to form a stiff dough; if dough is too dry, add a little water. Roll out dough 1/4 inch thick on a floured board. Cut into 4 inch squares. Arrange squares on a board, or pan, and dry until brittle. Gently boil a few squares of dough at a time in salted water until tender, 6 to 8 minutes. Drain well.

In a buttered baking dish, arrange successive layers of lasagna squares, tomato sauce, Mozzarella, and Parmesan cheese. Make at least three layers, using the ingredients in the same order. Bake lasagna in a 350 degree oven for 25 minutes.

Optional: This lasagna is specially good with shrimp. Cook, shell, and clean 2 lbs of shrimp and layer shrimp between the lasagna squares and tomato sauce.

Tabbouli

Tabbouli is the greatest middle eastern export since Omar Sharif.

2 cups bulgur wheat
8 cups boiling water
1 cup parsley, minced
1/2 cup fresh mint, finely chopped
1/2 cup green onions with 2 inches of tops, minced
2 large tomatoes, chopped
1/2 cup lemon juice
1/2 cup vegetable oil
1 Tbsp salt, or more to taste
1/2 tsp freshly ground pepper
3/4 tsp cinnamon

Put wheat into a mixing bowl and pour boiling water over it. Cover and let stand 2 or 3 hours, or until wheat is light and fluffy. Drain off excess water and shake wheat in a strainer until it is very dry. Add parsley, mint, green onions, and tomatoes.

Blend together lemon juice, vegetable oil, salt, pepper, and cinnamon. Pour over wheat and toss well. Chill for 1 hour.

Serve with Arab Bread. See page 6 6.

Vegetables rise to the occasion in this super souffle. Use any combination of vegetables you like.

3/4 cup zucchini, thinly sliced
1 cup cauliflower, broken into flowerets
1/2 cup fresh peas, shelled
4 carrots, diced
1 tsp vegetable salt
1/4 cup margarine
1/4 cup unbleached white flour

1 1/2 cups hot milk
2 Tbsp onion, grated
5 egg yolks, beaten
1/2 tsp salt
5 egg whites, stiffly beaten
3/4 cup mushrooms,
 sliced and sauteed

Steam zucchini, cauliflower, peas, and carrots until crisp-tender. Drain and season with salt. Cool.

Melt margarine in a skillet; add flour and stir for 1/2 a minute. Gradually add hot milk, stirring constantly until sauce thickens. Season sauce with onion. Cool.

Beat egg yolks into sauce and add salt. Fold in beaten egg whites, the cooled vegetables and sauteed mushrooms. Pour mixture into a greased souffle dish. Place dish in a pan of hot water and bake in a preheated 325 degree oven for 1 1/2 hours, or until souffle is well puffed and lightly browned.

Here's a beautiful spaghetti sauce to bring to a party—whether it's a friendly gathering or an encounter group.

1/4 cup olive oil
2 garlic cloves, minced
1 cup onions, finely chopped
3 1/2 cups ripe tomatoes, diced
2 cups tomato puree
1 cup tomato paste
1/2 cup water
1 tsp basil
1 tsp oregano
1/2 tsp sage
1 Tbsp vegetable salt
1 tsp ground black pepper
1 cup Parmesan cheese, grated

Heat oil and saute garlic and onions until tender. Add tomatoes, tomato puree, tomato paste, water, basil, oregano, sage, salt, and black pepper. Simmer 1 hour, stirring occasionally. Add more seasonings if necessary. Add Parmesan cheese, and simmer 30 minutes more.

Sex symbols, female activists, and ordinary chicks, all love a good soup. Serve this with a green salad and hunk of homemade bread. There's enough here to feed a small harem.

2 Tbsp vegetable oil
1 cup onion, chopped
1 cup carrots, chopped
1 cup celery, chopped
2 qts vegetable stock
1 1/2 tsp salt
1 bay leaf
1 tsp dill weed
3/4 cup pearl barley
2 1-lb heads firm cabbage, coarsely chopped
2 Tbsp parsley, minced
1/2 tsp ground black pepper
Sour cream

Heat oil in a skillet and saute onion, carrots, and celery until they're lightly brown.

Put vegetables into a large saucepan with vegetable stock, salt, bay leaf, dill weed, and barley. Cover and simmer soup 1 hour. The last 3 or 4 minutes add cabbage, parsley, and black pepper and simmer uncovered.

Before serving, spoon a big dollop of sour cream on top of each bowl of soup.

Polenta with Marinara Sauce 55

Polenta is an Italian peasant dish made from cornmeal and sparked with cheese and tomato sauce. Try it in your commune kitchen. The family will love it!

1 cup cornmeal
1 tsp salt
1 cup cold water
3 cups boiling water
1 cup grated Cheddar cheese or Parmesan cheese
2 cups Marinara sauce

Combine cornmeal, salt, and cold water; and blend well. Pour cornmeal into boiling water, and cook until mixture thickens in about 15 minutes. Stir frequently. Beat in Cheddar or Parmesan cheese. Pour into greased baking dish and let stand in a warm place for 10 minutes.

Spoon Marinara sauce over polenta before serving. Recipe for Marinara sauce is on page 53.

Optional: Add 1 cup of cooked, shelled shrimp to Marinara Sauce, and you have Shrimp Polenta—which is out of sight!

1/4 lb mushrooms, sliced
1/4 cup green onions, chopped
1/4 tsp garlic, minced
1 Tbsp vegetable oil
1/4 cup pureed tomatoes
1 1/2 tsp salt
1/2 tsp sugar
1/8 tsp black pepper
1/8 tsp marjoram
3/4 cup wholewheat pastry flour

1/2 tsp salt
1 tsp double-acting baking powder
2 eggs, beaten
2/3 cup milk
1/3 cup water
1/2 tsp vanilla or lemon juice
1/3 cup Parmesan cheese, grated
5 Tbsp margarine
Sour cream

Saute mushrooms, green onions, and garlic in vegetable oil for a few minutes. Add pureed tomatoes, salt, sugar, pepper and marjoram. Saute vegetables until liquid disappears. Reserve filling.

To make crepe batter, sift together flour, salt, and baking powder. Add eggs and beat in milk, water, and vanilla (or lemon juice) with a few swift strokes. Don't worry about any small lumps that may remain in the batter as they disappear in cooking. Pour 2 Tbsp of batter into a hot, lightly greased 6-inch skillet. Brown only one side of crepe. When crepe is cooked on the bottom, bubbles will form on top. Spoon 1 Tbsp of filling on uncooked side of crepe; roll up and place in a greased baking dish.

When you've finished rolling the crepes, sprinkle Parmesan cheese over the top and dot with margarine. Bake in a 350 degree oven for 15 minutes. Garnish with sour cream before serving.

Stuffed Summer Squash

Squash comes in all shapes and stuffings—this is one of the best.

2 lb summer squash	1/4 cup celery, chopped
1 cup cottage cheese	1/4 cup green onion, chopped
2 tsp pimiento, chopped	1/4 cup mushrooms, chopped
1/2 tsp vegetable salt	6 Tbsp margarine
2 eggs, beaten	1 cup Cheddar cheese, grated
1/2 tsp celery seed	Sour cream

Steam squash until crisp-tender. Cut off stem ends and scoop out center seeds leaving enough squash to provide a casing for stuffing.

In a bowl combine cottage cheese, pimiento, vegetable salt, eggs, and celery seed.

Saute celery, green onions, and mushrooms in 2 Tbsp margarine until tender. Stir into seasoned cottage cheese. Spoon stuffing into squash cases and dot with margarine. Sprinkle top with Cheddar cheese.

Place squash in baking pan with sufficient water to barely cover bottom of pan. Cover and bake for 10 to 15 minutes in a 400 degree oven. If you like, top each squash with 1 Tbsp of sour cream the last 5 minutes of baking. Serve with brown rice.

Another super stuffing can be made by combining 1 cup grated Cheddar cheese with 1/2 cup wholewheat bread crumbs, 1/2 cup chopped nuts, 1/2 tsp salt, 1/4 tsp pepper, 1/4 tsp paprika, a dash of Worcestershire Sauce, and sufficient melted margarine to moisten stuffing.

Optional: Shellfish may be added to the first recipe with tasty results.

Baja Beans

This lively chili from Baja, Mexico, can be fired up or fired down according to the flammability of your taste buds. Suit yourself on the spices.

1 lb kidney beans
2 cloves garlic, chopped
1 large onion, chopped
1 Tbsp salt
1 tsp crumbled red peppers
2 Tbsp chili powder
1/4 tsp black pepper
1 tsp cumin
1/2 tsp oregano
1/2 tsp paprika
1/2 cup tomato paste

Cover kidney beans with water; simmer for 2 minutes and remove from stove. Soak for 1 hour. Add garlic, onion, and salt—and more water to cover. Cover pot and simmer 1 hour. Season with red peppers, chili powder, black pepper, cumin, oregano, and paprika. Continue simmering beans another hour adding more liquid if necessary. Correct seasonings according to taste. Add tomato paste and simmer beans until very tender, stirring frequently.

Optional: Chicken is a savory addition to this chili. Poach, bone, and skin 2 chicken breasts. Cut into chunks and add to chili beans 20 minutes before beans are cooked.

Eggplant Macaroni

1/2 lb Vegeroni or regular macaroni
3 Tbsp margarine
12 slices eggplant, cut 1/2 inch thick
Unbleached white flour
1 cup vegetable oil
2 tsp vegetable salt
1/2 tsp black pepper

1/4 cup onion, finely chopped
*2 cups Vine Ripe Tomato Sauce
1 Tbsp parsley, finely chopped
1 tsp basil
1 cup Parmesan cheese, grated
12 1-inch squares Mozzarella cheese
3 Tbsp margarine, melted

Cook Vegeroni, or regular macaroni, according to directions on package. Drain well. Toss with margarine and keep warm.

Dip eggplant slices on both sides in flour. Heat 1/4 cup of vegetable oil and saute a few eggplant slices at a time, adding more oil to pan as required. When eggplant is brown on both sides, drain on paper towels. Season with salt and pepper.

Saute onion in remaining oil until tender and combine with Vine Ripe Tomato Sauce, parsley, and basil. Simmer 5 minutes.

Stir Vegeroni, or macaroni, into 1 1/2 cups of the tomato sauce and spoon a layer of sauce over the bottom of a shallow baking dish. Top with a layer of eggplant slices and a sprinkling of Parmesan cheese. Repeat, using remaining Vegeroni, or macaroni, eggplant slices, and cheese. Pour over remaining 1/2 cup of tomato sauce and top with Mozzarella cheese squares. Spoon over melted margarine.

Bake for 30 minutes in a 350 degree oven until top is golden brown and bubbly.

*For recipe for Vine Ripe Tomato Sauce see page 96.

Spinach-Ricotta Dumplings

These aren't the dumplings that grandmother used to make. They're light and delicious and digestible.

1 cup fresh, cooked spinach, chopped
1 1/2 cups Ricotta cheese
1 cup dry wholewheat bread crumbs, finely crumbled
2 eggs, beaten
1/3 cup Parmesan cheese, grated
1/4 cup green onions, minced
1 tsp salt
1 tsp basil
1/4 tsp nutmeg
Unbleached white flour
1 tsp salt
*2 cups Marinara Sauce

In a bowl combine spinach, Ricotta, bread crumbs, eggs, Parmesan cheese, onions, salt, basil, and nutmeg. Mix well. Form mixture into small finger-shaped dumplings about 2 inches long and 1 inch wide. Roll dumplings lightly in flour, Place on a foil-lined baking sheet in a single layer. Cover loosely with foil and chill for a few hours.

Pour 2 inches of water in a saucepan and add salt. Bring water to a gentle simmer and carefully poach 6 or 7 dumplings at a time. Dumplings will sink to the bottom of pan, but will rise to the top when cooked in about 4 or 5 minutes. Remove dumplings with a slotted spoon and keep warm on serving plate. Spoon Marinara Sauce over dumplings before serving.

*Recipe for Marinara Sauce is on page 53.

Mexican Carrot Soup with Guacamole

A dollop of Guacamole gives this carrot soup its olé.

4 carrots, sliced
1 onion, sliced
1 stalk celery, sliced
2 cups chicken stock or vegetable
   stock
1 tsp salt
1/4 tsp white pepper
3/4 cup half and half
1 avocado, mashed

1 Tbsp green onion, minced
1 tsp vegetable salt
1/2 tsp chili powder
1 garlic clove, crushed
Dash of Tabasco
1 Tbsp lime juice
1 ripe tomato, chopped
1/4 cup crushed tortilla chips

Combine carrots, onion, celery, and 1 cup stock in saucepan. Cover and simmer 20 minutes. Put vegetables and stock in a blender and puree vegetables—or put vegetables through a sieve. Add salt, pepper, and remaining stock and cream. Simmer soup in top of double boiler, over hot water, for 10 minutes; but do not let it boil.

In a bowl combine avocado, green onions, salt, chili powder, garlic, Tabasco, lime juice, tomatoes, and torilla chips.

Pour soup into bowls, and just before serving, add a heaping Tbsp of Guacamole on top as a garnish. Serve with homemade tortillas.

FLOUR POWER

Bread is money. Bread is friendship. Bread is also grain—whole, natural grains that nourish and flavor.

It is the freshness of the flour that gives bread its power. Aside from using unbleached, whole grain flours, it is important that all your baking ingredients be fresh, including the yeast. Fresh active dry yeast, which should be kept in the refrigerator the same as your flour, is very sensitive to temperatures. It works best when dissolved in lukewarm or tepid water no hotter than 80 degrees for compressed yeast, or 110 for powdered.

In Mexico, yeast doughs are called *almas,* or souls, because they seem so spirited. To produce a lively dough, it must rise slowly for 1 or 2 hours, then be punched down and allowed to rise again for another hour in the baking pan. The rising process can't be rushed, so allow time for this little miracle.

Baking bread is a celebration of life and a sharing of the heart. Enjoy it!

Herb Bread

Herbs enhance most foods—especially this bread.

1 package of fresh, active dry yeast
1/4 cup warm water
3/4 cup milk, scalded
2 Tbsp sugar
1 1/2 tsp salt
2 Tbsp vegetable margarine

1 egg, beaten
1/2 tsp nutmeg
1 tsp powdered sage
2 tsp celery seed
3 cups sifted, unbleached white
  flour

Dissolve yeast in warm water. Combine scalded milk with sugar, salt, and margarine. Cool mixture to lukewarm. Add yeast and stir well. Add egg, nutmeg, sage and celery seed. Stir in 2 cups of the flour and beat until dough is smooth. Gradually stir in remaining cup of flour, or sufficient flour to make a workable, soft dough.

Knead dough from 5 to 8 minutes on a lightly floured board until smooth and elastic. Place dough in a greased bowl and turn so it is oiled on all sides. Let rise until it doubles in size in about 1 1/2 hours. Punch dough down and leave it for 15 minutes.

Shape dough into a round loaf and place it in a greased 8 inch pie pan. Let dough rise again until it doubles in size. Bake in a preheated 400 degree oven for 35 to 40 minutes.

Buttermilk Pound Cake

An old fashioned, honest-to-goodness pound cake that's worth its weight in flavor.

1/2 cup vegetable margarine
2 cups raw sugar
4 eggs
3 cups unbleached white flour
1/4 tsp baking soda
1 cup buttermilk
2 tsp vanilla
1 tsp almond extract
2 Tbsp lemon peel, grated
2 Tbsp orange peel, grated

Beat margarine and sugar together until creamy. Beat in eggs, 1 at a time, until mixture is smooth.

Sift together flour and baking soda. Beat into margarine-sugar mixture alternately with buttermilk. Stir in vanilla, almond extract and grated lemon and orange peel.

Pour batter into greased and floured loaf pans. Bake in a 350 degree oven for 1 hour until cake is a rich brown.

Freckle Bread

Freckle bread has more freckles than Tom Sawyer. The "freckles" are tasty raisins stirred into the batter.

2 packages fresh, active dry yeast
1 cup warm water
1/2 cup lukewarm mashed potatoes
8 Tbsp raw sugar
5 1/4 cup unsifted, unbleached
   white bread flour

1 tsp salt
2 eggs, beaten
1/2 cup margarine, melted and
   cooled
1 cup dark seedless raisins

Sprinkle yeast into water; stir until dissolved. Add mashed potatoes, 2 Tbsp sugar and 1 cup flour. Beat until smooth. Cover and let rise until bubbly, about 30 minutes. Stir, adding remaining sugar, salt, and 1 more cup flour. Beat until smooth. Stir in eggs and margarine. Add raisins. Stir in enough additional flour to make a soft dough.

On a lightly floured board, knead dough until smooth and elastic. Place in a greased bowl, turning dough around so it is greased on all sides. Cover. Let rise in a warm, draft-free place until dough has doubled in size. Punch down and divide into 4 parts.

Shape each part into a slender loaf about 9 inches long. Place 2 loaves side by side in greased 9 x 5 inch loaf pans. Let rise until doubled in size. As the loaves rise, they will meld together forming one loaf. Bake about 50 minutes in a 350 degree oven. Recipe makes 2 loaves.

Arab Bread

1/2 cup warm water
2 packages fresh, active dry yeast
1/4 tsp sugar
6 cups unbleached white flour

3 Tbsp olive oil
2 tsp salt
2 cups warm water

Combine warm water with dry yeast and sugar. Stir until yeast dissolves and begins to work a little. Leave for 5 minutes.

Sift flour into a mixing bowl. Add olive oil, salt, and warm water and stir well with a wooden spoon. Beat in dry yeast mixture until thoroughly blended.

Turn dough onto a floured board and knead for about 10 minutes until dough is smooth, and no longer sticky. Oil a bowl and turn dough in the bowl on all sides so it is coated with oil. Cover and let rise in a warm place until dough doubles in size in about 2 hours.

Punch dough down, and knead for 3 minutes. Roll and stretch out dough into a thick sausage roll about 15 inches long and 3 inches wide. Cut roll into 15 equal size pieces; pat each piece into a ball. Roll out each ball into circles 6 inches in diameter and 1/8 inch thick.

Place circles on pieces of foil paper and let stand at room temperature for 1 hour more until the dough rises again.

Preheat oven to 500 degrees so it is very hot. Leave the dough circles on the pieces of foil and put directly into the hot oven on the lowest shelf. Bake 3 to 5 minutes until bread puffs up and browns. Don't overcook or it will burn. This bread is delicious hot; or, you can use it later for sandwiches or whatever.

Onion Flat Bread

This bread is cooked in a skillet Russian style.

2 onions, minced
6 Tbsp margarine
1 tsp salt
3/4 cup warm water
3 cups wholewheat pastry flour

Saute onions, in 2 Tbsp margarine until they're tender but not brown. Dissolve salt in water.

Melt remaining margarine and combine with water and onions. Cool.

Sift flour and gradually add onion liquid, working the liquid into the flour until it no longer sticks to your fingers. Add a little more flour or a little more liquid to get the right consistency to the dough.

Form dough into a ball, cover with a towel and let rest for 1/2 hour. Divide dough into individual balls 1 1/2 to 2 inches in diameter. On a lightly floured board, roll out dough balls into thin circles of dough about 7 or 8 inches in diameter.

Heat an ungreased skillet and brown bread on both sides for 10 minutes or so. Dry bread circles on a rack.

Coffee Can Bread

An empty coffee can makes a handy baking pan for round bread—which is easier to swallow than square bread.

2 Tbsp fresh, active dry yeast
1/2 cup warm water
1 cup milk
2 Tbsp margarine
2 Tbsp molasses
1 tsp salt
1 egg, slightly beaten
1 cup rolled oats (or other whole grain cereals)
1 3/4 cups wholewheat flour
1 3/4 cups unbleached white bread flour

Dissolve yeast in water.

Scald milk and add margarine. Cool to lukewarm. Stir in molasses, salt and egg. Add milk mixture to yeast and stir in rolled oats. Mix flours and beat in flours gradually, using about 400 strokes—until dough is very elastic.

Let dough rise in a greased, covered bowl for 1 hour.

Punch dough down and place in a well-greased 2 lb empty coffee can. Cover and let dough rise in a warm place for another hour.

Bake in a 350 degree oven for 1 hour and 15 minutes until top forms a crusty, well-browned dome. Cool bread in can for 15 minutes before removing.

Homemade Bread Sticks

These delicious bread sticks can be enjoyed anytime, anywhere—while hitch-hiking, bike riding, or while doing your Yogi exercises.

1 package of fresh, active dry yeast
2/3 cup warm water
1 tsp salt
1 Tbsp raw sugar
1/4 cup vegetable margarine, softened
2 cups unbleached white flour
1 egg
1 Tbsp water
Sesame seeds, poppy seeds, celery seeds, cornmeal or coarse sea salt

In a mixing bowl dissolve yeast in warm water. Add salt, sugar, margarine, and 1 cup flour. Beat well until smooth. Gradually add remaining cup of flour, and knead dough on a floured board until smooth. Put into a bowl, cover, and let dough rise for 1 hour until it doubles in size.

Divide dough in half. Cut each half into 24 pieces. Roll out each piece of dough into a 6 inch pencil-slim stick. Place sticks on a greased baking sheet 1 inch apart. Brush with egg beaten with 1 Tbsp water. Sprinkle sticks with a mixture of sesame seeds, poppy seeds, celery seeds, and cornmeal or coarse sea salt.

Bake bread sticks in a 350 degree oven for 20 to 25 minutes until golden brown.

Eve's Apple Bread

This is hearty enough to serve as bread, yet fancy enough to pass for cake.

1/2 cup vegetable margarine
1 cup raw sugar
2 eggs, beaten
1/4 cup water
2 cups unbleached white flour
1 tsp baking soda
1/2 tsp salt
1/2 tsp ground cloves
1 tsp cinnamon
2 cups apples, pared and finely chopped
2/3 cup walnuts, chopped

Cream together margarine and raw sugar. Add eggs and water and stir well. Sift together flour, soda, salt, cloves and cinnamon. Beat into sugar-egg mixture, and add apples and walnuts.

Spoon into a greased 9 inch loaf pan. Bake in a 350 degree oven for 1 hour. Cool bread in pan before removing.

Try this date nut bread with some homemade cream cheese. It's right on!

1 1/2 cups boiling water
2 tsp baking soda
1 cup pitted dates, finely chopped
2 eggs, beaten
6 Tbsp vegetable oil
1 1/2 cups raw sugar
3 cups wholewheat flour
1 tsp salt
2 tsp baking powder
1 tsp vanilla
1 cup walnuts, shelled and coarsely chopped

Pour boiling water over soda and mix well. Add dates. Cool. Stir in eggs.

Blend vegetable oil with sugar. Sift together flour, salt, and baking powder; and blend with oil-sugar mixture. Add date-egg mixture, vanilla and walnuts. Stir well and pour batter into a greased loaf pan.

Bake in a 350 degree oven for 1 hour. Cool loaf before cutting.

Carrot Wedding Cake

A cake for all celebrations of life.

2 cups raw sugar
3 cups wholewheat pastry flour
1 tsp baking soda
1 tsp baking powder
1/2 tsp salt
1 cup vegetable oil
4 eggs, beaten
3 cups grated carrots

1/2 cup walnuts or pecans, chopped
1/2 cup raisins
1/2 cup pitted dates, chopped
1 cup bananas, mashed
1/2 cup coconut, finely chopped
1 cup fresh crushed pineapple
1 tsp vanilla
1 tsp cinnamon

Sift together sugar, flour, baking soda, baking powder, and salt. Beat in vegetable oil and eggs. Stir in carrots, nuts, raisins, dates, bananas, coconut, and pineapple. Season with vanilla and cinnamon.

Grease a shallow rectangular baking pan about 12 x 9 inches and a shallow pan about 9 x 8 inches. Pour cake batter into both pans and bake in a 325 degree oven for 1 hour. Let cake cool in pans for 45 minutes; remove and spread with the following icing:

1 cup powdered sugar
12 oz cream cheese, softened

Beat cream cheese and sugar together until smooth. Spread icing over top and sides of each cake layer; center the smaller layer on top of the larger layer.

FAR OUT PICNICS

Picnics are far out. They float up to the sky in hot air balloons and go down to the sea in ships. They move as fast as a Honda or slow as a hike.

Thanks to thermal containers, picnics go anywhere and keep their cool—or stay as hot as you like.

The vegetarian picnic is a great improvement over the Great American Hot Dog. It utilizes all of nature's summery fruits and vegetables in luscious salads, sandwiches, soups—and even barbecues. Here are some out-of-sight ideas for the picnic basket.

Have a nice day—and leave the scenery as nice as you found it!

The best picnics just happen—like a nice day. They're put together with ingredients you pick up en route at a roadside produce stand, health food store, of if need be, a supermarket.

Vegetable Garden Salad

This Vegetable Garden Salad combines a lot of crunchy vegetables in a yogurt dressing. It can be mixed in a plastic bag which also serves as a salad bowl.

Wash, cut, and combine the following vegetables: 2 tomatoes, quartered; 1 cucumber, sliced; 2 zucchini, thinly sliced; 1/4 lb raw mushrooms, sliced; 1 cup broccoli flowerets; 2 carrots, thinly sliced; 2 green peppers, seeded and sliced; 1 bunch green onions, sliced; and 4 radishes, sliced.

Toss salad in a plastic bag with 1 cup yogurt which has been blended with 1 tsp honey, 1/2 tsp vegetable salt, 1 tsp lemon juice, and a little grated lemon rind.

Cut 2 avocados in half and remove pits.

In a plastic bag mix together: 1/3 cup of fresh washed alfalfa sprouts, 4 sliced green onions, 1/3 cup sour cream, 1/2 cup cottage cheese, 1 tsp vegetable salt, and 2 tsp lemon juice.

Spoon salad into avocado halves before serving.

GREAT PUT-ONS
FOR SANDWICHES

Honest bread made from whole grains is a picnic in itself; but when you want to build a sandwich, try these groovy fillings:

Combine cream cheese or cottage cheese with chopped dates, dried fruits, chopped nuts or sunflower seeds. Very tasty.

Cream cheese is also neat with chopped watercress or alfalfa sprouts.

Try this weird combo: grated Cheddar cheese, chopped pimientos, green onion, celery, and a dab of sour cream.

Mix together a little sour cream, lemon juice, basil, vegetable salt, and chopped parsley. Spread dressing over two slices of bread and top with a thick slice of tomato and red onion.

My favorite put-on: slices of avocado, Swiss cheese, and sweet red onion, on pumpernickel.

PICNICS THAT MAKE THE SCENE

Whatever the scene—rock festival or sports rally—it's a good idea to bring your own food, if you don't want to go the route of the nearest hamburger joint. The moveable feast can be as small as a stuffed egg and fancy as a casserole. We give you recipes for both—along with some thermos soups, and a hero-sized sandwich.

Picnic Casserole

Wash 1 lb fresh spinach and 1 lb Swiss chard. Remove stems and chop vegetables finely.

Heat 2 Tbsp olive oil in a skillet and saute vegetables briefly until they are wilted. Remove spinach and chard, and add 5 diced zucchini, 2 diced tomatoes. 1 chopped onion, 1 clove of garlic, and 1 Tbsp basil.

Saute vegetables for 10 minutes or until lightly cooked. Remove garlic. Season with 1 Tbsp vegetable salt, and 1/2 tsp black pepper.

Spoon vegetables into a greased baking dish, together with the spinach and chard.

Beat 8 eggs until light and foamy, and combine with 1 tsp salt. Pour eggs over vegetables.

Combine 1/2 cup grated Parmesan cheese with 1/2 cup wholewheat bread crumbs, and sprinkle over top of baking dish. Dot with 3 Tbsp of margarine.

Bake casserole in a preheated 400 degree oven for 20 minutes, or until eggs are set and the top is fairly firm.

This dish is as good hot as cold—if you want to have a picnic in your pad.

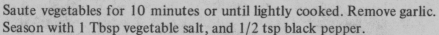

Blender Tomato Soup

Combine in a blender: 12 large ripe tomatoes (the riper the better), 6 green chopped onions, 1 Tbsp vegetable salt, 1 tsp sugar, 1/2 tsp marjoram, 1/2 tsp thyme, 2 Tbsp lemon juice, and 2 tsp grated lemon rind. Blend vegetables until ingredients are pureed. Stir in 1 1/2 cups sour cream, 1 tsp curry powder, and 1 Tbsp chopped parsley.

Chill in refrigerator until icy cold before pouring into a thermos.

Cold Mexican Rice Salad

Combine 2 cups cold cooked brown rice with 1 cup thinly sliced, seeded green pepper, 2 small sliced pimientos, 2 tomatoes cut in strips, 6 sliced green onions, and 2 chopped hard-cooked eggs.

Blend together 1 tsp marjoram, 1/2 tsp basil, 1 Tbsp chopped parsley, 1/4 cup vegetable oil, 1/4 cup olive oil, 1/4 cup wine vinegar, 1 tsp vegetable salt, and mix well.

Pour dressing over rice salad, and toss well.

Vegetable Chowder

Melt 5 Tbsp margarine and saute 1 cup shredded lettuce, 1 cup finely chopped celery, 1 chopped onion, and 2 chopped carrots for 5 minutes. Add 5 cups vegetable stock and 1/2 cup fine noodles broken into 2 inch lengths. Cover pot and simmer for 20 minutes. Season with salt and pepper to taste and simmer another 10 minutes. Pour into wide-neck thermos.

Stuffed Eggs with Almonds

Remove yolks from 6 shelled, hard-cooked eggs; and mash yolks with a fork. Add 4 Tbsp mayonnaise, 1/4 tsp salt, 1 tsp brown mustard, and 3 Tbsp chopped, salted, and roasted almonds.

Fill egg cavities with almond mixture. Press whole almond on top of each egg half.

Wrap eggs securely in foil paper and keep chilled.

Oriental Stuffed Eggs

Remove yolks from 6 shelled hard-cooked eggs and mash with a fork. Add 3 Tbsp mayonnaise, 1/2 tsp soy sauce, 2 Tbsp chopped green onion, and 3 Tbsp finely chopped water chestnuts.

Fill eggs with mixture and top each egg half with a sprig of parsley. Wrap eggs in foil and keep chilled.

Continental Hero Sandwich

Buy, or bake, a loaf of good chewy French bread with a hard crust. Cut bread in half lengthwise, and rub inside with a split clove of garlic. On one half of the loaf, put 5 or 6 slices of Jack cheese; 3 slices of peeled red onion, separated into rings; 3 large, ripe sliced tomatoes; 3 whole pimientos, cut in half; and 8 or 10 black, pitted olives which have been sliced. (Greek or Italian olives are the tastiest.)

Sprinkle vegetables with 1 Tbsp olive oil, 1 Tbsp wine vinegar, and season with 1/2 tsp basil, 1/2 tsp oregano, and 1/2 tsp vegetable salt.

Top with other half of loaf, and slice loaf into equal portions for 4 or 6 people.

If you want to vegetate in the wilderness, try these easy vegetable barbecues which are simply prepared and devoured. They're grilled in individual foil packets, one to a customer.

Eggplant

Cut a square of heavy duty foil paper large enough to enclose a slice of eggplant, a slice of onion, a slice of tomato, and a large mushroom, sliced. Season vegetables with 1/2 clove crushed garlic, 1/4 tsp pepper, 1/2 tsp basil. Drizzle 2 Tbsp olive oil over vegetables. Bring up sides of foil square and fold together overlapping folds tightly. Seal well and grill packet over medium coals for 1 hour. Turn packet frequently. Sprinkle vegetables with 1/2 tsp vegetable salt and serve in the individual packets.

Corn on the Cob

Remove husks and silk from fresh corn. Spread each ear of corn with margarine. Sprinkle with 1/4 cup grated Cheddar cheese. Wrap corn in heavy duty foil and grill 6 to 8 inches from slow burning coals for 15 to 20 minutes. Turn corn every 5 minutes while roasting. Season with vegetable salt before serving.

Place a thin slice of peeled potato in the center of foil square and top with a thin slice of tomato and a thin slice of onion. Season with 1/4 tsp pepper, 1 Tbsp chopped parsley and 1 Tbsp margarine. Add another layer of potato, tomato and onion and a pat of margarine and 1/2 tsp basil. Wrap up foil packet tightly and grill over medium coals for 1 1/2 hours. Season with vegetable salt before serving.

Vegetable Kebabs

Skewer small whole onions, cherry tomatoes, green pepper squares and whole small mushrooms. Brush with vegetable oil, seasoned with crushed garlic, pepper and herbs. Grill 5 minutes over slow coals. Season with vegetable salt. Serve roasted vegetables on toasted French bread or sour dough roll with some cooked brown rice to go with it.

MUNCHIES FOR PEACEFUL DEMONSTRATIONS

Picnics happen anywhere—even at a protest rally. There's nothing that whets the appetite more than a peaceful demonstration. These pocket-sized snacks are nourishing, and easy to munch on the run!

The World's Greatest Cereal Snack

Combine in a mixing bowl 3 cups of raw, quick-cooking rolled oats, 1/2 cup unsweetened wheat germ, 1/4 cup sesame seed, 1/2 cup flaked coconut, 1/2 cup chopped almonds or pecans, 1/3 cup raw sugar, 1/2 tsp salt and sprinkle with 1 1/2 tsp vanilla. Mix well and spread cereal out on a baking pan in a thin layer.

Bake at 275 degrees for 50 to 60 minutes. Mix and stir mixture every 10 minutes. Cool.

Add 1 cup raisins to cereal and stir. Spoon out the amount of cereal you want to take with you into plastic sandwich bags. Store the rest of this cereal snack in an air-tight container.

Salted Soybeans

Wash and soak dry soybeans overnight.
Cook beans in water to cover for 1 hour.

Drain and dry beans. Spread beans on a baking sheet and pour over sufficient soy oil to coat beans, and sprinkle with salt.

Bake in a moderate 350 degree oven for a couple of hours. Stir beans frequently.

Apple 'N Cheese

Wash, core, and slice a tart apple in 1/4 inch horizontal slices.

Dip slices in lemon juice to prevent discoloration.

Slice Cheddar cheese in 1/4 inch slices, and place between apple slices.

Wrap tightly in foil.

Sesame Munchies

Blend 1 cup wholewheat flour with 1/4 cup vegetable oil. Add 1/2 tsp salt, and about 2 Tbsp of ice water, or just enough to make a dough the consistency of piecrust.

Chill dough and roll out 1/8 inch thick on a floured board. Cut into finger-width strips about 1 inch wide and 3 inches long.

Place strips on a greased baking sheet. Sprinkle strips with 1/2 cup sesame seeds, pressing them into the dough. Bake in a 350 degree oven for 10 minutes or until strips are golden brown.

DOWN HOME KITCHEN

Before supermarkets, groceries came from the down home kitchen. Food was freshly prepared from the bounty of the farm; preserves were homemade and butter hand-churned.

The return to organic cooking has produced a new down home kitchen. Making your own relishes, dairy products, and sauces, is not only tastier but more fun.

Our down home kitchen covers classic staples from homemade noodles to peanut butter—as well as the groovey foods like bean sprouts and yogurt. There are also right on vegetable sauces and salad dressings.

Put on your grannie glasses, fire up your built-in stove, and try these down home recipes!

HOMEMADE DAIRY PRODUCTS

You don't have to have a cow to make these dairy products, only a little patience. Wait until you try this Russian-style sour cream—which is richer, thicker, and tastier than the commercial product.

We would like to emphasize that any dairy foods—as well as sauces, relishes, or other perishable foods kept in jars—must be stored in sterilized, airtight containers. All foods should be refrigerated—with the exception of the dairy products below requiring fermentation before chilling.

How To Sterlize Containers

Wash jars and lids in hot soapy water before using, and rinse well. Place jars on a rack in a large pot and add water to cover. Bring water to a boiling point. Reduce heat and simmer 10 minutes.

When you're ready to use jars, remove from water with a pair of tongs, drain, and fill containers promptly making sure lid is tightly turned.

Sour Cream

Pour 1/2 pint of heavy cream into a sterilized container, and add 2 1/2 tsp buttermilk. Pour in another 1/2 pint of heavy cream and close container.

Leave in a warm place 12 to 24 hours, or until cream thickens. Chill before using.

Yogurt

Heat 1 qt of milk to lukewarm temperature. Stir in 2 Tbsp of store-bought yogurt to use as a starter. (Once you make your own yogurt, save a little to use as a starter for the next batch.) Stir milk and yogurt until well blended; pour into a sterilized container and cover.

Set container in a pan of hot water until container is submerged to within a few inches from the top. Let stand for 6 to 8 hours in hot tap water and replace water as it cools off.

When milk curdles and solidifies like a creamy pudding, it has turned to yogurt. Chill before using.

Cream Cheese

Pour 1 pint of cream into a sterilized container, cover, and leave cream for a few days until it sours.

Pour contents into a cheesecloth bag and let it drain. When all liquid drains out, season cheese with 1 tsp salt.

Mix well and shape into squares before chilling.

Cottage Cheese

Pour 1 qt milk into a saucepan and heat it to lukewarm. Add 2 tsp of lemon juice per cup of milk (or 8 tsp) to sour milk quickly. Stir well.

Pour into sterilized jar, cover, and leave all day.

When milk is thoroughly curdled, strain it through cheesecloth, pressing out the whey with a wooden spoon to drain cheese thoroughly.

Season with vegetable salt to taste and refrigerate.

HOMEMADE CONDIMENTS
AND
RELISHES

Add life to your spice—make it yourself. This homemade curry fires up some great dishes.

Curry Powder

Mix together 2 Tbsp ground turmeric, 2 Tbsp crushed cumin seeds, 2 Tbsp crushed coriander seeds, 1 Tbsp ground ginger, 1 Tbsp black ground pepper, 2 tsp crushed cardamon seeds, 2 tsp ground mace, 1 tsp crushed mustard seeds, and 1 tsp ground cloves. If you wish to make this curry a little hotter, increase the amount of ginger or pepper.

Gomasio (Sesame Salt)

Gomasio is the table salt of the macrobiotic diet; however, it's a flavorful seasoning for any cookery. Gomasio is made from 1 part sea salt to 5 parts toasted sesame seeds.

First, toast the salt until it is crystalline and sparkling. Grind the salt in a mortar until powdered.

Rinse sesame seeds in a strainer and toast them in a skillet until evenly browned. Add sesame seeds to mortar and grind them together with the salt until both are powdery and completely mixed.

Make only a little of this sesame salt at a time, enough for a week's supply, and keep it in an airtight jar away from moisture or heat.

Seasoned Salt

Mix together 1 cup sea salt, 1 tsp ground black pepper, 1/2 tsp cayenne, 1/2 tsp mace, 1/2 tsp marjoram, 1/4 tsp powdered cloves, 2 tsp dry mustard, 2 tsp curry powder, 3 Tbsp paprika, 3 tsp garlic salt, 1/2 tsp celery salt, and 1 Tbsp parsley flakes.

Peach Chutney

Finely chop together 1 onion, 1 clove garlic, and 1 cup seedless raisins.

In a large kettle combine chopped onion mixture with 1 qt peeled, chopped peaches, 1 Tbsp chili powder, 1/4 cup chopped crystalized ginger, 1 Tbsp mustard seed, 1 Tbsp sea salt, 1/2 tsp cinnamon, 1/2 tsp nutmeg, 1/2 tsp allspice, 1/2 tsp ground cloves, 1 cup cider vinegar, 1 cup water, 1 cup raw sugar, and 3 Tbsp molasses. Bring contents to a boil and stir until sugar is dissolved. Reduce heat and simmer, uncovered, until mixture is quite thick and deep brown, in about 45 minutes.

Ladle chutney into hot, sterilized jars. Cool and store in refrigerator.

Summer Vegetable Relish

Combine 1/4 cup wine vinegar, 3/4 cup salad oil, 1 Tbsp sugar, 1 garlic clove, slivered, 1/4 tsp ground black pepper, and 1/2 tsp paprika. Mix well.

In a bowl, mix together 3/4 cup pimiento-stuffed olives, 1/2 cup chopped celery, 3/4 cup diced cauliflower, 1/2 cup diced carrots, 1/2 cup diced white turnips, 1/2 cup small white onions, 1/2 cup chopped green pepper, 1/2 cup diced summer squash, and 1/4 cup chopped pimientos.

Pour dressing over vegetables and marinate in refrigerator for 48 hours before using.

Mexican Hot, Hot Salsa

In a blender, combine 5 seeded green chilies, 1 small chopped onion, 2 cloves garlic, 1/2 tsp coriander, 1 Tbsp vinegar, 1 Tbsp olive oil, and 1/2 tsp sea salt.

Blend ingredients at high speed until finely chopped. Add 5 chopped, very ripe tomatoes. Blend until smooth.

If you like a sauce that is less fiery, cut down on the number of chilies, and use the canned green chilies which are less flammable than the fresh.

These are two basic soup stocks. Take your pick according to what food trip you're on—vegetarian or semi-vegetarian.

Vegetable Stock

Almost anything goes to make a rich vegetable stock: tomatoes, onions, lettuce, watercress, leeks, carrots, or whatever vegetable parings you have. However, use the strong flavored vegetables like turnips or broccoli with a light hand.

Here's one of my favorite vegetable soup stocks: In 2 qts water put 1 cup sliced carrots, 1 cup sliced celery (including leaves), 1/2 cup shredded spinach, 1/2 cup shredded lettuce, 1 large chopped onion, 1 large chopped celery root, 2 tomatoes quartered, 1 Tbsp chopped parsley, 1 tsp basil, and 2 Tbsp vegetable salt (or more according to taste). Cover and simmer stock for 30 minutes to 1 hour.

Strain broth, cool and store in refrigerator. (If you're on a macrobiotic diet, eliminate the tomatoes.)

Chicken Stock

Place 4 lb of chicken wings, backs, and necks in a pan; and roast them in a 400 degree oven until they begin to brown. Drain off fat.

Place chicken in a large saucepan with 2 qts water. Bring water to a boil and skim off foam. Cover and simmer chicken 1 hour. Add 1 chopped leek, 2 celery stalks with leaves, 1 chopped onion, 1/4 cup chopped parsley, 1 large bay leaf, 3 whole peppercorns, 1 Tbsp salt, and 1/2 tsp paprika. Simmer another hour.

Strain soup stock; cool, and store in refrigerator. When ready to use, remove fat which has risen to surface, and strain through 2 layers of cheesecloth.

HOMEMADE VEGETABLE SAUCES

It's good to have a repertory of fresh, savory sauces to vary your vegetable dishes. The source and scorcery of many a sauce is bechamel.

Bechamel Sauce

Melt 4 Tbsp margarine in a saucepan.

Remove from heat and stir in 4 Tbsp unbleached white flour.

Return pan to heat and cook margarine and flour mixture over low heat for 1 minute. Slowly add 1 1/2 cups milk, stirring constantly. When sauce reaches boiling point, stir in 1/2 cup cream, 1 tsp salt, and 1/4 tsp white pepper. Simmer another 1/2 minute until sauce thickens.

Fresh Mushroom Sauce

Saute 1/2 cup sliced mushrooms in 2 Tbsp margarine for 5 minutes. Add 2 Tbsp unbleached white flour and stir. Gradually add 1 1/2 cups half-and-half, and stir until sauce thickens. If you like, season sauce with 2 Tbsp dry sherry.

Sour Cream Cheese Sauce

In a double boiler melt 1 cup sharp grated Cheddar cheese with 2 Tbsp margarine. Stir in 1/2 cup sour cream, and salt & pepper to taste. 1 tsp of fine herbs, or any seasoning you desire, may be added to this sauce.

Mornay Sauce

Melt 1/4 cup margarine in a skillet, and stir in 1/4 cup unbleached white flour.

Remove from fire and stir well.

Return to stove and gradually add 1 3/4 cup of half-and-half, salt & pepper to taste, and 1/4 tsp nutmeg. When sauce thickens, add 1/2 cup grated Parmesan and Gruyere cheese mixed together.

When cheese melts, remove sauce from fire and add a few Tbsp of sauce to 2 beaten egg yolks. Stir egg yolks back into sauce.

Try this sauce for dishes which are quickly browned in the oven, or under the broiler; it makes a beautiful topping.

Aioli Sauce

Mash 1 small cooked and peeled potato until smooth. Mash in 2 crushed cloves of garlic, and 2 hard-cooked egg yolks which have been put through a sieve. Mix well. Beat in 3 large egg yolks. Gradually beat in 2 cups vegetable oil, 3 Tbsp lemon juice, and salt & white pepper to taste.

This sauce has the consistency of mayonnaise and is excellent with both hot and cold vegetables, as well as fish.

Sour Cream Herb Sauce

Melt 2 1/2 Tbsp butter in a skillet and combine with 1 Tbsp grated onion. Blend in 2 1/2 Tbsp unbleached white flour. Slowly stir in 1/2 cup light cream, and cook until sauce is smooth. Stir in 1 cup sour cream, 1/2 tsp salt, 1/4 tsp paprika, 1 Tbsp chopped chives, 1 tsp chopped parsley and 1 tsp basil. If you like curry, add 1/2 tsp curry powder.

Blender Hollandaise

Put 3 egg yolks in a blender with 2 Tbsp lemon juice, 1/2 tsp salt, and 1/2 tsp white pepper. Turn blender on and off to mix seasonings and yolks.

Melt 3/4 cup margarine in a saucepan until very hot but *do not brown.*

Turn blender on to high speed and pour hot margarine slowly but steadily into blender. Blend for 1 minute or until sauce thickens.

Japanese Teri-Yaki Sauce

In a saucepan combine 10 Tbsp of soya sauce with 15 Tbsp of mirin, or Japanese rice wine.

Simmer sauce over a low flame until about 1/3 of the sauce evaporates.

Teri-Yaki is great for basting chicken and fish as well as an accent for vegetables.

Vinaigrette Sauce

Combine 4 Tbsp wine vinegar, 1 cup olive oil, 1/2 cup chopped parsley, 2 Tbsp chopped chives, 1 Tbsp chopped capers, 2 Tbsp chopped green onion, 1/2 tsp dry mustard, 2 hard-cooked chopped eggs, 2 tsp salt, and 1 tsp pepper.

Mix ingredients and let stand at room temperature a few hours.

This is delicious over cold cooked asparagus, broccoli or green beans, or when used as a dip for cold cooked artichokes.

Margarine Sauce Seasonings

Add any of the following seasonings to melted margarine before spooning over vegetables: parsley, dry mustard, mint, lemon juice, grated onion, garlic, sauteed mushrooms, celery salt, freshly grated nutmeg, grated lemon or orange rind, paprika, chives, fresh or dried herbs, curry powder, Worcestershire Sauce, horseradish, chopped watercress, chopped bean sprouts, toasted chopped nuts, caraway seeds, poppy seeds, or toasted sesame seeds.

The lively flavor of tomato is one of the most versatile and frequently used seasonings in the kitchen. It enriches casseroles, vegetables, pasta, soups, or whatever you like. This luscious, homemade tomato sauce is fresh from the vine.

Vine Ripe Tomato Sauce

Heat 3 Tbsp olive oil in a skillet and add 1 large, finely chopped onion, 1/2 green pepper, seeded and chopped, 2 finely chopped ribs of celery including leaves, 1 chopped carrot, and 1 minced clove of garlic. Saute vegetables for 5 minutes. Add 6 large, very ripe finely diced tomatoes.

Season sauce with 1/2 bay leaf, 1 tsp raw sugar, 2 sprigs fresh parsley, 1 tsp basil, 1/2 tsp oregano, 2 tsp vegetable salt, and 1/2 tsp pepper. Add 1/2 cup water or vegetable stock. Simmer sauce for 45 minutes, stirring frequently.

Correct seasonings and put sauce through a sieve before pouring into sterilized jars. Keep in refrigerator.

Fresh Tomato Paste

In a large saucepan combine 6 lbs of fresh, very ripe, chopped tomatoes with 2 Tbsp basil, 2 tsp vegetable salt, 1/2 tsp pepper, 3/4 cup
chopped celery, 3/4 cup chopped carrots, and 1 large chopped onion.
Simmer vegetables on a low heat until they are very soft and tender.
Press vegetables through a sieve. Simmer vegetables for another hour
or until sauce becomes a thick paste. (It's good to use an asbestos pad
over the burner to keep heat low.) Be sure to stir sauce frequently to
keep it from burning.

HOMEMADE
SALAD DRESSINGS

Here are a few of my favorite embellishments for greenery.

French Dressing

Combine 1/4 cup olive oil, 1/3 cup salad oil, 1/4 cup wine vinegar or lemon juice, 1 tsp honey, 1 clove garlic cut in half, 1 tsp salt, 1/2 tsp paprika, 1 tsp dry mustard, and 1/4 tsp ground black pepper. Place ingredients in a jar and shake well. Add 1 Tbsp of chopped fresh or dried herbs, if you like.

Avocado French Dressing

Peel 1 very ripe avocado and mash pulp until smooth. Stir in 2 Tbsp mayonnaise, 1/2 cup French dressing, 1/2 tsp vegetable salt, and a dash of paprika.

Blender Mayonnaise

Combine 2 eggs, 2 Tbsp lemon juice, 1 Tbsp white vinegar, 1/2 tsp dry mustard, and 1 tsp salt in a blender. Cover and blend at high speed for 30 seconds. Slowly drizzle in 1 1/2 cups salad oil. Blend until thick and smooth.

Cheese Dressing

Combine 1 cup homemade mayonnaise with 2 tsp Worcestershire Sauce, 1/4 cup grated Cheddar cheese or crumbled Roquefort cheese or 1 package softened cream cheese. Blend well.

Yogurt Dressing

Combine 1 cup yogurt, 2 Tbsp lemon juice, 1/2 tsp dry mustard, 1/2 tsp salt, 1 tsp paprika, 1 minced clove garlic, 2 Tbsp grated onion, and 1 Tbsp chopped chives.
Chill in the refrigerator a few hours before using.

Caraway and Cottage Cheese Dressing

Combine 2 chopped radishes, 2 hard cooked mashed egg yolks, 1/3 cup cottage cheese, 1 Tbsp chopped green pepper, 1 minced garlic clove, 1 tsp caraway seeds, 1 tsp salt, 1/2 tsp paprika, 2 Tbsp lemon juice, and 1/2 cup buttermilk. Mix well.

Honey Lime

Combine 1 cup homemade mayonnaise, 1/2 cup honey, 1 cup whipped cream, and 1/4 cup lime juice. Blend ingredients and chill. Try this on fruit salads. Beautiful.

Chutney East

Combine 1 hard-cooked, chopped egg, 2 Tbsp chopped chutney, 1/2 tsp curry powder, 1 Tbsp lemon juice, 1/2 cup salad oil, 3 Tbsp wine vinegar, 1/4 tsp salt, 1 tsp sugar, and 1/4 tsp black pepper. Stir well with a fork before serving.

Sour Cream Dressing

Beat 1 egg yolk with 1/4 cup sour cream. Gradually beat in 1/2 cup French dressing. Season with 1 tsp lemon juice, and 1 Tbsp chopped fresh dill (or 1 tsp dried dill weed) and 1 Tbsp chopped parsley.

As any connoisseur of the noodle will tell you, the best are homemade.

Beat together 3 egg yolks and 1 whole egg until eggs are very light. Beat in 4 Tbsp cold water and 1 tsp salt. Add 2 cups of sifted, unbleached flour and knead dough with your hands.

Divide dough into 3 parts. Roll out each part into a very thin sheet on a floured board. Cover with a towel and let stand 30 minutes.

Roll up dough like a jelly roll, and with a sharp knife cut into desired noodle widths. Lay out noodles on a baking sheet to dry well. They may be used immediately or stored.

Green Noodles

Stir together in a bowl 4 cups of unbleached white flour, together with 1 tsp salt. Make a well in center of flour, and put in 3/4 cup of well-drained *spinach puree, and 2 large, well-beaten eggs. Knead dough with your fingers until all ingredients are well mixed; dough should be stiff, but if it's too dry, add a little water.

Divide dough into 3 parts. Roll out each part into thin sheets on a floured board. Roll up sheets like a jelly roll and slice into narrow strips. Spread strips on a pan and leave until dry and brittle before using.

*To make spinach puree, steam leaves for 5 minutes until soft and wilted. Place spinach in blender with 1/8 cup of liquid rendered from steaming. Blend on low speed and add more liquid if puree seems too dry.

HOMEMADE NOODLE SAUCES

This Pesto Sauce from Genova makes a flavorful topping over both kinds of noodles—as well as spaghetti.

Pesto Sauce

Combine in a mixing bowl 1/4 cup dried basil or 1/2 cup fresh basil, 1/4 cup fresh chopped parsley, 1 clove of crushed garlic, 1/4 tsp salt, 1/3 cup shelled pine nuts or walnuts finely ground, 1 cup freshly grated Parmesan cheese, and 1 Tbsp margarine. Mash ingredients well, adding 1/4 cup of olive oil, a little at a time, until sauce has the consistency of creamed butter. If necessary, add a little more olive oil.

Toss sauce well with hot, drained noodles, or spaghetti; add 2 Tbsp of margarine and toss again before serving.

Cream Cheese Noodle Sauce

Steam 1 cup of finely chopped celery until celery is just tender. Drain.

Melt 2 Tbsp margarine in a skillet and stir in 2 Tbsp unbleached white flour. Gradually add 2 cups hot milk. Add 6 oz of cream cheese and stir until cheese melts. Season with 1 tsp salt, and 1 tsp fine herbs. Add 1/2 cup chopped black olives and celery, and simmer another 1/2 minute.

Serve over hot, drained white noodles.

MORE
DOWN HOME IDEAS

Grinding your own peanut butter isn't really a grind—the blender does all the work.

Homemade Peanut Butter

Sprinkle 2 cups raw shelled peanuts with 2 tsp salt. Place on baking sheet and roast in a 400 degree oven for approximately 15 to 20 minutes, stirring every 5 minutes.

Grind up nuts in a blender; add 1 1/2 to 2 Tbsp peanut oil or vegetable oil until it is blended to a dry paste. Add 1 tsp honey, 1/2 tsp almond extract, and 1 tsp granular lecithin (available in health food stores).

Cream all ingredients together and store in refrigerator.

Homemade Tortillas

Mix 2 cups masa harina flour with 1 1/3 cups warm water, and 1 tsp salt. Mix ingredients to form a soft dough.

Divide dough into 12 small balls. Press and pat each ball between two sheets of wax paper; roll with rolling pin to form 6 inch circles. Or, if you have "Mexican palms," pat out the dough with both hands into tortilla-sized circles. If the tortillas stick, the dough is too moist and you need to add a little more masa harina. If the dough is too dry and keeps falling apart when you work with it, add a little more water.

Cook one tortilla at a time in an ungreased griddle over medium heat, about 2 minutes on each side; or fry them in a lightly oiled skillet. Place a sheet of wax paper between tortillas as you make them.

To keep tortillas warm, wrap them in paper towels, then in cloth which had been wrung out in hot water. Then wrap in foil paper and keep in slightly warm oven.

Homemade Seasoned Bread Crumbs

Leave 4 slices of wholewheat bread out in the air overnight until bread is dry and stale.

Crumble bread and put into a blender; blend for a few minutes until crumbs are finely crumbled. Mix crumbs with 1 tsp thyme, 1/2 tsp basil, 1/2 tsp tarragon, and any other herbs you desire. Season with 1/2 tsp garlic salt, 1/2 tsp celery salt, 1/2 tsp paprika, and 2 Tbsp minced parsley.

Grow Your Own Bean Sprouts

It doesn't take any real estate to sprout your own soybeans or alfalfa seeds. Here's the way:

Sort beans, or seeds, and remove any broken ones or bits of stems and leaves. Wash beans, or seeds, and soak overnight in lukewarm water to cover. Drain.

Place beans or seeds in the bottom of a wide-mouth bottle or jar, allowing sufficient room in container for beans to double in size. Cover mouth of container with cheesecloth or screen and fasten securely with a rubber band. Cover with a damp cloth so all light is excluded. Beans must be kept dark and moist. Water beans several times each day. Each time invert jar to drain beans or seeds thoroughly.

Sprouts are ready to eat when they're about 1 1/2 to 2 inches long.

Homemade Bean Curd or Tofu

Soak 1 cup soybeans overnight in water to cover.

Grind beans in a food chopper or blender.

Boil beans in 6 cups water for 5 minutes. Lower flame, cover pot, and simmer for 15 minutes. Drain mixture, or chaff, in strainer.

The liquid you'll get is called soybean milk. Pour into sterilized container. Cover, and let soybean milk stand in warm place until it thickens. Separate the thickened curd from the rest of the liquid, and put it into a pan with water to cover. Simmer for 5 minutes.

Remove curd and drain through a cheesecloth. Season with salt. Cut into pieces.

Make Your Own Refried Beans

(Frijoles Refritos)

We close with a great down home or down casa recipe for refried beans.

2 cups pinto beans or red kidney
    beans
2 onions, finely chopped
2 cloves garlic, chopped
2 bay leaves
1 tsp dried red chilies or 2 tsp chili
    powder
4 Tbsp vegetable oil
Salt to taste
1/2 tsp ground black pepper
1 large ripe tomato, chopped

Wash beans and place in saucepan, without soaking, with enough cold water to cover. Add 1 onion, 1 chopped garlic clove, bay leaves and dried chilies or chili powder. Cover beans and bring to a boil; reduce heat and simmer gently, adding more boiling water as it boils away. When beans begin to wrinkle, add 1 Tbsp oil. Continue cooking until beans are soft. Stir in salt to taste and pepper.

Cook 30 minutes more, but do not add water as there should be a minimum of liquid when beans are cooked.

Heat remaining 3 Tbsp of oil and saute remaining onion and chopped garlic. Add tomato and simmer for 2 minutes.

Remove skillet from stove and add 3 Tbsp of beans to onions and tomato with some liquid from bean pot. Mash ingredients until you have a smooth heavy paste. Mash all but 1/2 cup of remaining beans.

Combine mashed and whole beans and simmer 20 minutes over low heat, adding more vegetable oil if needed. Beans should be creamy.

These refried beans make a hearty filling for tacos when combined with a strip of Jack cheese and a strip of green chili pepper. Try them for bean burritos, too. A burrito is a flour tortilla rolled and stuffed with whatever is handy—meat, beans, etc.

INDEX

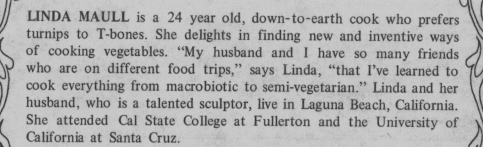

LINDA MAULL is a 24 year old, down-to-earth cook who prefers turnips to T-bones. She delights in finding new and inventive ways of cooking vegetables. "My husband and I have so many friends who are on different food trips," says Linda, "that I've learned to cook everything from macrobiotic to semi-vegetarian." Linda and her husband, who is a talented sculptor, live in Laguna Beach, California. She attended Cal State College at Fullerton and the University of California at Santa Cruz.

Nancy Fair McIntyre is a journalist and the author of five cookbooks. Her culinary adventures range from Roman banquets to the macrobiotic rice bowl. She lives in Laguna Beach, California, with her husband who is a publisher, and her daughter Megan.